JESUS
Man to Man

A Devotional for Men

Achieving powerful victory
through a conversation with
the one man who knows

By, Warren Peterson

Copyright Notices:

JESUS Man to Man

© 2018 Warren Peterson

Table of Contents

Introduction:

It's often easy to forget that Jesus was a man. We can get so focused on him being the Son of God that we lose the reality that he was also the human son of Joseph and Mary and that he was a man.

And like all other men, he faced hard times, trials, and challenges. He had bad days. He had exhausting days. He had days where he just wanted and needed some quiet down time away from everyone. He had days where he just wanted some time alone with his friends to recharge.

Just like you.

Jesus was born, he grew up from a baby to a toddler, to a young boy, to a teenager, to a young man, to the man that changed the course of human history.

Jesus worked hard, after all, he was a carpenter. And that meant hard manual labor, with his hands.

Jesus would have been lean and strong, as his work would have demanded. He would tire from carrying and working with heavy stone and wood.

Jesus would get dirty, he would get cuts, and scrapes, and bruises. He would get slivers in his hands. He would accidentally drop stone on his foot. He would get sweat in his eyes, and he would ache after a long day of work.

Jesus would have to deal with irritated customers, projects with unclear expectations, and with unrealistic deadlines. He would have to get up and go to work on days where he may have preferred to do something else.

Just like you.

One day when I was thinking about Jesus, as a man, I started to wonder, what would it be like to just sit down and talk with him, man to man? Would he be able to really relate to the struggles and challenges that men living today are dealing with? Would he be able to connect with me, and the life I'm living right now? Would he be able to answer all the questions I have?

In this book, I attempt to answer those questions. I want to be very clear, I'm writing to you with the words, the tone, and the concepts that I feel the holy spirit has moved me to share with you.

Because of that, this was a challenging book for me to write in the first place, something you may notice in the questions as you read along. After all, who am I to presume to write something like this?

I'm just a man walking the walk of life. I've not attended seminary. I have lots of my own problems and challenges. I don't claim to have some magic formula for living a perfect life. I've made lots of mistakes and continue to make mistakes all the time. I'm just, well... me. The idea that I would put words in the mouth of Jesus was intimidating, to put it mildly. This same idea nearly stopped me many times while writing.

However, I felt strongly compelled that this should be the next book I write. Every day as I sat down at the keyboard to write what you are about to read, I first prayed for guidance, wisdom, insight, and the words to share with those of you who have chosen to read along. I prayed that God would use this work to lead others to know him and to build a relationship with Jesus.

I thank you for reading this book and ask for your grace as you move through these pages. It's my sincere desire that you find words that will help you on your journey through life, that you find answers to some of your own questions, and that you come to connect with Jesus on a whole new level.

Now, let's get started!
-Warren

Important Note – Since this book is written from the viewpoint of Jesus sitting down and having a conversation with me, man-to-man, and talking about men and men's issues, corresponding masculine language is used in the questions and the answers.

Clearly there are very many points throughout this entire book which apply to women one hundred percent equally as they do to men. So with that being said, if you're a woman who is reading along, thank you for your understanding of this point. I hope you get much from this book, even though the language is written for men, and from a man's perspective.

Reading Suggestions

As you read through these pages, I'd like you to do more than simply read the sections and move on with your day. I'd like you to actively be involved with what you read, to study what is written, to revisit sections for review, and to spend time each day thinking about how Jesus would want you to integrate what you read.

Here are some suggestions for your reading:

1. Focus on the scriptures provided for each section, considering how they apply to your life, right now.

2. Pray about how you can use what you're reading, and about how you can share what you're learning with others.

3. Take the time to answer the questions that have been provided, use them as prompts for further notes.

4. Write down your ideas, thoughts, prayers, and action items for each section.

5. Get together with other men and discuss each section. Support and encourage one another. Challenge one another.

6. Share your thoughts with Jesus. Start your own, perhaps for the first time, conversation with him.

7. Implement what you learn into your life. Become the man you were created to be.

Key Bible Verses for This Book

Despite all these things, overwhelming victory is ours through Christ, who loved us. *Romans 8:37*

Iron sharpens iron, and one man sharpens another. *Proverbs 27:17* (ESV)

For I can do everything through Christ, who gives me strength. *Philippians 4:13*

Show yourself in all respects to be a model of good works, and in your teaching show integrity, dignity, and sound speech that cannot be condemned, so that an opponent may be put to shame, having nothing evil to say about us. *Titus 2:7-8* (ESV)

Therefore, put on every piece of God's armor so you will be able to resist the enemy in the time of evil. Then after the battle you will still be standing firm. *Ephesians 6:13*

I have fought the good fight, I have finished the race, and I have remained faithful. *2 Timothy 4:7*

And be sure of this: I am with you always, even to the end of the age. *Matthew 28:20*

Be watchful, stand firm in the faith, act like men, be strong. Let all that you do be done in love. *1 Corinthians 16:13-14* (ESV)

STARTING WHERE YOU ARE

I want to begin with this. Often, when there is a change I know I need to make, I will talk myself out of it. I'll use the excuse that I'm not yet ready to start. I'll tell myself that I have to do more research, or that I have to get some other project done first. I'll create some reason why now can't work out. How can I push past my excuses and know when I'm ready to start?

Jesus: Other than starting where you are now, what other choice do you have? You can't go back in the past and start earlier, so your time is right now. As the old saying goes, the best time to plant a tree was twenty years ago, and the second-best time to plant a tree is today.

Those excuses happen because you don't yet believe in yourself. You use those excuses to justify inaction and to stay where you are. It's safer to stay where you are, even if you know it isn't the right place for you to stay.

Although you may not yet believe in yourself, I believe in you. I know what kind of great man you can become, and I want to see you become that man.

Once you know me, once you come to me, once you believe in me the way I believe in you, you're starting a brand-new phase of your life. You are literally made new again, ready to fulfill the plans that have been created for you. While you don't yet know where your life will take you, the Father does. And he has designed good and hopeful plans for you.

In your plans, make sure that you include time in your day, every day, for prayer about the projects you are working on and the ones you're about to start. Allow the Father to provide you with wise council on your choices.

When you're feeling down, come to me so I can have your back. When you're feeling that your changes are not going the way you want them to, come to me so I can lift you up. Your time to start is right now. You're ready right now. So, get to work and make those changes!

Scriptures:

Isaiah 43:18 "But forget all that – it is nothing compared to what I am going to do."

Jeremiah 29:11 "'For I know the plans I have for you,' says the Lord. 'They are plans for good and not for disaster, to give you a future and a hope.'"

2 Corinthians 5:17 "This means that anyone who belongs to Christ has become a new person. The old life is gone; a new life has begun!"

Questions: What has stopped you from starting? Are you ready to be open-minded and challenged in new ways? Have you allowed your excuses to prevent you from improving yourself?

PREPARING FOR BATTLE

So, following on that, why is it that so many men, right when they start something important or new, or right when they begin to really make changes in their lives, hit so many roadblocks? Why is it that the hard times seem to come right after I've decided to improve?

Jesus: These roadblocks and hard times come because every man is facing a battle, and every man is in the middle of the fight. I want more men to realize that this battle is taking place, as too many pretend it isn't or ignore it entirely. This battle is not on the physical battlefield, rather it's in your inner self, in your mind, and in your heart. That's where your real battle is happening.

There's an enemy who seeks to keep you down. This enemy is a liar and a murderer; he is the evil one who seeks to crush your spirit and make you retreat into the shadows. Your enemy wants you to become a small and broken man.

It's not a coincidence that right when you seek to improve is right when the challenges come. That's a direct attack on you, on your family, and on your future. Recognize it for what it is. The trial you're facing is not a random event, but an assault on your own growth and improvement.

Even now, as we're talking the attack will come. You'll question and doubt what I'm sharing with you. You'll wonder if what I'm saying can be true. That's all part of the battle you're fighting, right now.

When you seek to improve, that enrages your enemy. When you seek to rise above the struggle, that enrages your enemy. Your enemy doesn't want to see you ever improve or change for the better.

But I do! I want you get into the fight. I want you to stand firm against the attack. Don't fear this battle, because with me you can succeed. With me, you can improve. With me, you can triumph over your challenges.

I will strengthen you, and when you feel like you are under attack come to me. I am waiting for you with open arms, and I will always have your back.

Scriptures:

Ephesians 6:10-12 "A final word: Be strong in the Lord and his mighty power. Put on all of God's armor so that you will be able to stand firm against all strategies of the devil. For we are not fighting against flesh-and-blood enemies, but against evil rulers and authorities of the unseen world, against mighty powers in this dark world, and against evil spirits in the heavenly places."

1 Timothy 6:12 "Fight the good fight for the true faith. Hold tightly to the eternal life to which God has called you, which you have declared so well before many witnesses."

Philippians 4:13 "For I can do everything through Christ, who gives me strength."

Questions: Do you recognize the challenges for what they really are? Did you realize there is an enemy who is actively working against you? Do you go to Jesus during those times of trial?

VICTORY TOGETHER

The times when I've had the hardest problems in my life, were the times when I felt the most alone. In our society now, many men feel like they need to do everything on their own, and that it's showing weakness to count on anyone else. I know that I've felt that way myself at times before, as if everything was on my shoulders to figure out by myself. Is it wrong to try and do that, to try and be the one figuring it all out?

Jesus: First know that no one man has it all figured out, no one man has all the answers. Every man will experience how life is hard, how life has trouble, and how life has serious times of challenge and struggle. During those times, if you're trying to have it all figured out by yourself, you're at serious risk of falling into a pit of anxiety, depression, or worse.

The enemy likes to make men think they are, or they must be, on their own all by themselves when walking through those trials. This is one of the lies that he whispers into the ears of all men, and it's a lie that men have to recognize.

Times when you're alone are times when you're vulnerable, when you'll listen to the lies, when you'll start to believe the lies, and when you can find yourself pulled down in a spiral of pain and confusion. You must stand against the lie, and one of the most powerful ways you can do that is with another man by your side.

When you're standing with an ally by your side, someone who will speak the truth and lift you when needed, not only can you hold fast and defend your position, but you can advance and defeat the troubles in your life. In other words, you and your ally can go on offense to win the fight.

More powerful still is when you and your ally bring me in, as the third man of your group, as we then form a strong bond that's not easily broken. When we're together, you stand strong against the enemy's attacks. When we're together, you achieve victory.

Scriptures:

Galatians 6:2-3 "Share each other's burdens, and in this way obey the law of Christ. If you think you are too important to help someone, you are only fooling yourself."

Philippians 2:2 "Then make me truly happy by agreeing wholeheartedly with each other, loving one another, and working together with one mind and purpose."

1 Thessalonians 5:10-11 "Christ died for us so that, whether we are dead or alive when he returns, we can live with him forever. So encourage each other and build each other up, just as you are already doing."

Ecclesiastes 4:12 "A person standing alone can be attacked and defeated, but two can stand back-to-back and conquer. Three are even better, for a triple-braided cord is not easily broken."

Questions: Who is the man you can go to, right now, who will share your burdens? Who are the men who can come to you and share their burdens? What does achieving victory over the enemy's attacks look like, in your life?

SEX

OK, let's get right to one of the topics that's most frequently on the mind of lots of men, and that's sex. In the Bible, you don't directly talk much about this, so what are some of your thoughts on sex between a husband and wife?

Jesus: Ha, I love it - I bet lots of guys will go to this section first! I'm not surprised a man asks this right away, and I'm happy that we got into talking about sex early. Listen, God the Father created male and female; he created sex in the first place. Sex between a husband and wife should be an amazing, beautiful, and wonderful thing. Sexual intimacy brings a couple together physically, emotionally, and spiritually.

Sex is a regular part of a healthy marriage. It's the husband's job to make sure his wife's sexual needs are satisfied, and it's the wife's job to make sure her husband's sexual needs are satisfied. Neither the husband nor the wife should withhold sex from their spouse, as the sex drive is very powerful and having needs go unmet can lead to inappropriate thoughts and to marriages that crumble.

Fighting against sexual thoughts and impulses is one of the more difficult challenges for most men, and it's important that they do fight against those desires. One reason this is such dangerous territory is that sexual thoughts can quickly lead to actions that can quickly destroy families, churches, and entire communities. Sex really is that powerful, and men must guard their hearts and their minds when it comes to their sexual thoughts. Men's sexual thoughts are to remain for the romance and beauty of their wives.

I want to add how much I love the Song of Songs book; it's such poetry, such romance, and so beautiful. I know that the analogies don't use your language today but imagine if they did! That book teaches a man that he shouldn't just demand quick sex from his wife, but rather he should learn how to take the time to woo her, to love her, and to appreciate her. Men that talk about not knowing how to romance a woman; they should take a page out of Solomon's playbook!

Scriptures:

Matthew 19:4 "Haven't you read the Scriptures?" Jesus replied. "They record that from the beginning God made them male and female."

1 Corinthians 7:3 "The husband should fulfill his wife's sexual needs, and the wife should fulfill her husband's needs."

1 Corinthians 7:5 "Do not deprive each other of sexual relations, unless you both agree to refrain from sexual intimacy for a limited time so you can give yourselves more completely to prayer."

Song of Songs 4:16 "Awake, north wind! Rise up, south wind! Blow on my garden and spread its fragrance all around. Come into your garden, my love; taste its finest fruits."

Questions: How are you making sure that your wife's sexual needs are met? In what ways are you guarding your heart and your mind against dangerous sexual thoughts? No matter how long you've been married, are you wooing and romancing your wife?

MARRIAGE

I have several friends that are about to get married. They are young, and just starting out on this next part of their lives. And I have other friends who have been married for decades. What advice do you have for these men about marriage?

Jesus: When a man and woman are married, they're brought together in a unique way, unlike any other relationship between people. They are truly joined together, two individual people now united as a team of one. They're to work together, to support one another, and to grow in life together.

As a married couple, they are to set an example for others to see. They are to love one another, and to experience joy and intimacy together. They are to be open with and have no fear with one another.

Keep in mind that when the ways of the world get involved, things can get complicated. Instead of heeding my teaching, instead of working towards supporting one another, and instead of being joined together as a team, they can be pulled in opposite directions.

The pull of career, of paying bills, and other disagreements can make it so the vows they took long ago seem like a quaint memory of the past, instead of the lighthouse they were intended to be.

Holding fast to the commitments made to each other, with God as a witness, must remain a priority in the marriage, otherwise, those ways of the world will feel stronger and stronger.

Marriage vows do not call for a specific career. They do not call for a specific size house. They do not call for a specific bank account. In fact, most vows state just the opposite. They state support for richer, for poorer, in sickness and in health. When the challenging times of life come, and they will, remember the vows made to one another.

Lastly, when the Father is actively brought into the marriage, when He is the team captain, then the marriage is stronger and stronger. Think of how strong a big rope is when it is braided from three individual ropes; a marriage with God at the center is like that braided rope. It is very, very strong.

A marriage where the husband and wife are committed to God first and committed to one another second will be a powerful union for all to see.

Scriptures:

Matthew 19:5 "And he said, 'This explains why a man leaves his father and mother and is joined to his wife, and the two are united into one.'"

1 Peter 4:8 "Most important of all, continue to show deep love for each other, for love covers a multitude of sins."

Ecclesiastes 4:12 "A person standing alone can be attacked and defeated, but two can stand back-to-back and conquer. Three are even better, for a triple-braided cord is not easily broken."

Questions: Are you still committed to your wedding vows? When did you last read/watch your own vows? Is God the team captain of your marriage?

MAN NEEDS WOMAN

In our culture today, there is a movement of men, including men who have been hurt by women, choosing to go through life without women. These men have made the decision that it is better to be alone than have a woman by their side, due to the potential consequences that can happen in that relationship. Why is it not good, if that is the truth, for a man to be alone?

Jesus: While there are always exceptions, it's not good for a man to be alone. Even Adam, who had a perfect union with and was in constant communication and relationship with God himself, was told by God that it wasn't good for him to be alone.

When Adam had this perfect relationship with God, he was still not at ease. He was still longing for a partner, just as he noticed all the rest of creation was in pairs and that there was none other like him. And to that, God created woman to live with the man.

After the Father had created Adam, but before he had created woman, he stated the situation was not good. His response to fixing that not good situation was to create woman. In other words, Adam and Eve, when joined together, changed the entire situation from not good to good. In his own words, the Father's creation was not good until Eve was in the picture. That's how important women are!

Men are made for relationships; relationship with me, relationship with the Father, relationships with friends, and the exclusively intimate, powerful, and important relationship between a husband and wife. A man learning to put other people's needs, including his own wife's, ahead of his own is an important step in building that relationship.

A husband who has a wife is a man who doesn't go through life alone, as he has that unique relationship in his life. A husband who has a wife has someone to provide him with the help he needs, as he walks through life. A husband who has a wife has someone for a close and intimate sexual connection, one he need never be ashamed of and which allows for them to create new life.

Just as Adam and Eve were created to be together, men today are created to be with women.

Scriptures:

Genesis 2:18 The Lord God said, "It is not good for the man to be alone. I will make a helper suitable for him."

Proverbs 18:22 "The man who finds a wife finds a treasure, and he received favor from the Lord."

Matthew 19:6 "Since they are no longer two but one, let no one split apart what God has joined together."

Questions: What are your thoughts on the fact that the creation of Eve changed Adam's situation, from God's perspective, from one that was not good to one that was good? If you're married, what can you do to remember that your wife is a treasure?

LUST

As much as I'd rather not admit it, there are times when I admire the shape and beauty of a woman other than my wife for a bit too long, or when I have lustful thoughts in my mind. I then end up feeling guilty and feeling shame, but those feelings never stop it from happening again. How do I get control over those thoughts and this problem?

Jesus: Lust is something that all men, to one level or another, have to deal with in their lives. It's one of the challenges that nearly all men have in common. And it doesn't matter if you have everything in life, or you have nothing in life, lust is an area of temptation for all men.

Even King David fell from lust. He saw a beautiful woman, lusted after her, and the enemy used his lust to corrupt his heart. Remember, this was a man who had everything, at least according to the world, and his lust led him to commit adultery and even arrange the death of the woman's husband.

On the other end of the spectrum was Joseph. When he had nothing, after being sold into slavery, he finds himself in the home of a powerful man, a man whose wife had her eyes set on Joseph. When the powerful man's wife was tempting Joseph, even to the point of physically grabbing him and demanding to have sex with him, he knew he had to get out of there. He didn't stay and think about the pros and cons; he simply ran from the room.

Like Joseph, it's good for you to know that you should run from those situations. You need to be willing to run from anything that you can feel is corrupting your heart. It could be as minor as turning your head away from lustful sights, or it could be as major as you physically leaving a situation.

It's also good for you to know what and who you should run towards at these times. When you notice lust creeping into your heart, run to the Father. Talk with me, bring your heart to the Father. I want you to ask for forgiveness and then let go of the guilt and the shame that you feel. Once you have made the choice to ask for forgiveness, it's time for you to continue on to the next step of your journey. Choose to intentionally change what you're thinking about and choose to talk with me instead.

Scriptures:

2 Timothy 2:22 "Run from anything that stimulates youthful lusts. Instead, pursue righteous living, faithfulness, love, and peace. Enjoy the companionship of those who call on the Lord with pure hearts."

Proverbs 6:25 "Don't lust for her beauty. Don't let her coy glances seduce you."

Genesis 39:12 "She came and grabbed him by his cloak, demanding, 'Come on, sleep with me!' Joseph tore himself away, but he left his cloak in her hand as he ran from the house."

Colossians 3:5 "So put to death the sinful, earthly things lurking within you. Have nothing to do with sexual immorality, impurity, lust, and evil desires. Don't be greedy, for a greedy person is an idolater, worshiping the things of this world."

Questions: How will you run from situations or media that are leading your heart down the path of lust? In what ways will you change your focus towards Jesus?

WAKE UP

I've had many times, years even, where I have just gone through the motions. I've done what I believed everyone wanted me to do. I've acted the way people have told me I should act. I've followed the lead that I thought I was supposed to follow. And every time I do that, I'm miserable inside. I still look the part on the outside, but inside I'm screaming every day. How do I break out of a mindset like that?

Jesus: There's a problem with men in your culture, and your question is an example of this problem. You found yourself walking through life, but still sleeping. You found yourself doing things all day long, but never truly awake. As a man, you need to wake up.

The world wants you to remain asleep, just going through the motions day after day, year after year. Because when you're doing this, you're not focused on me, on the Father, or on your calling. When you remain busy doing everything the world is wanting you to do, you miss out on the big picture and don't get to work on what the Father has called you to do.

Your enemy likes it when you remain asleep. Your enemy likes it when you sedate yourself through overworking, through addiction, through sports, through pornography, through remaining alone, or through anything that keeps you sleeping and not awakened to who you could become.

To get out of that mindset, you need to first recognize that you're sleeping. You need to realize that there's more for you in this life, and that it won't be easy to get there. You need to be willing to consider new things, new ideas, and stretch yourself in ways you haven't before. You need to live with the light that I provide and live to become an example to the world of who a wide-awake man is.

You need to pray to the Father, asking him to show you the way forward. Pray for wisdom. Pray for forgiveness. Pray for guidance. Pray for direction. Pray for him to open your eyes so that you can truly see who you can become. Pray to wake up.

Scriptures:

Romans 13:11-12 "This is all the more urgent, for you know how late it is; time is running out. Wake up, for our salvation is nearer now than when we first believed. The night is almost gone; the day of salvation will soon be here. So remove your dark deeds like dirty clothes, and put on the shining armor of right living."

Ephesians 5:14 "For the light makes everything visible. This is why it is said, 'Awake, O sleeper, rise up from the dead, and Christ will give you light.'"

1 Thessalonians 5:6 "So be on your guard, not asleep like the others. Stay alert and be clearheaded."

Questions: Which ways are you sedating yourself today, so that you aren't fully awake? In which areas of your life (marriage, parenting, faith, health, etc..) do you need to wake up?

PRAYER

I must admit that I feel inadequate in my praying. I tend to pray the same things; I have consistent prayers of gratitude and appreciation, but often feel like I'm not praying "right" or not praying "good enough". Is there a right way to pray?

Jesus: No, there is no one right way to pray in all situations. Prayer is one of the ways for you to communicate with me, to improve your relationship with me, to better know the Father, and to build your faith.

Prayer isn't just about asking for what you want and need in your life, although you should share those thoughts with the Father. It's about receiving the strength to do the will of the Father. It's about building our relationship together, just as you talk with your fellow men to build a relationship with them. It's about more than that, but that's a great starting point for where we are today.

Since there isn't a right way to always pray, how you pray is less important to me than the fact that you do pray to the Father. I want you to communicate with him, to share your life with him, to talk about your hopes, dreams, struggles, and challenges. I want you to open up to me about your life. I want you to ask for forgiveness when you make mistakes. I want you to express gratitude for your blessings. I want you to pray with faith in knowing that the Father is listening.

Men often overlook the listening side of prayer. When you are praying, sometimes the best thing you can do is be quiet and listen. That doesn't mean you will always hear a direct response, but you need to give time for the Father to reply back to you.

There also isn't a right time to pray; prayer can be anytime day or night. Prayer can be formal, like in a church setting, or it can be informal, like a man driving by himself on the open road. Some of the most powerful prayers are from men who are out on a hike or drive by themselves, with no distractions and with them simply sharing what is on their heart.

Prayer need not be complicated or intimidating. Simply talk to the Father; he's listening, right now.

Scriptures:

1 Peter 5:7 "Give all your worries and cares to God, for he cares about you."

Ephesians 6:18 "Pray in the Spirit at all times and on every occasion. Stay alert and be persistent in your prayers for all believers everywhere."

Psalm 17:6 "I am praying to you because I know you will answer, O God. Bend down and listen as I pray."

Romans 8:26-27 "And the Holy Spirit helps us in our weakness. For example, we don't know what God wants us to pray for. But the Holy Spirit prays for us with groanings that cannot be expressed in words. And the Father who knows all hearts knows what the Spirit is saying, for the Spirit pleads for us believers in harmony with God's own will."

Questions: How often do you pray to Jesus? Are there parts of your life that are off limits in your prayers? When you pray are you only asking for things, or are you seeking to share your life with Jesus?

WISDOM

We live in confusing times. We have more information in the palm of our hands than ever before. The Internet has given us access to nearly any piece of information we want, in an instant. Why does it seem that with all this knowledge, there is less wisdom than ever before?

Jesus: Knowledge is obviously wonderful, the things that people have figured out about the Universe, and the things that they are about to figure out, are truly amazing. There are some people studying and ready to make incredible discoveries as we speak.

However, people have confused knowledge with wisdom, when they are not the same thing. One can possess immense knowledge of the world and yet have little wisdom. While at the same time one can possess little knowledge, and yet be the wisest man on Earth.

This lack of wisdom leads directly to the confusion you see in the world. This lack of wisdom means that men make unwise choices, without any awareness of the true consequences of their choices. This lack of wisdom leads men to do things, say things, and act in ways opposite of what I have taught, causing confusion and chaos.

Many in this world have chosen to ignore my teaching, which is as if they built their homes on the sand in a dry river bed. So, when the rain comes in, when the floodwaters rise, their homes are washed away. Building a life based on knowledge, instead of based on my teaching, is like building a home on sand instead of solid rock.

No matter how much knowledge a man might gain, no matter how much information he has access to if he's not building his life on the wisdom of what I have explained, he hasn't built his life on a solid foundation, which means that challenges can quickly destroy his home. Such a man needs more wisdom, the wisdom I offer.

And if a man is wise enough to know he is lacking wisdom, all he must do is ask the Father for more. God will provide opportunity after opportunity to increase wisdom.

Scripture:

Matthew 7: 24-27 "Anyone who listens to my teaching and follows it is wise, like a person who builds a house on solid rock. Though the rain comes in torrents and the floodwaters rise and the winds beat against that house, it won't collapse because it is built on bedrock. But anyone who hears my teaching and doesn't obey it is foolish, like a person who builds a house on sand. When the rains and floods come, and the winds beat against that house, it will collapse with a mighty crash."

James 1:5 "If you need wisdom, ask our generous God, and he will give it to you. He will not rebuke you for asking."

Questions: Where are you pursuing knowledge instead of wisdom? Have you built your life on the sand, or on the solid rock found in Jesus?

FORGIVENESS

When it comes to forgiveness, I have a specific struggle. Somewhere, in the back of my mind, I have equated forgiving someone with me saying that what they did was ok after all.

For example, I was discussing this with a pastor, and he asked me if I could forgive the 9/11 hijackers. That really stuck with me, as my immediate answer was, No! Not a chance. How could I forgive them, after all the evil, death, pain, and suffering they personally caused? I wanted them, and anyone associated with them, to be brought to justice, not "just forgiven".

In my mind, I had been making the connection that when I forgive someone, that somehow, I'm fully pardoning them, and like I said, that what they did was ok. I think this isn't right, but how do I look at this differently?

Jesus: Now this one is tough. Lots of people struggle with this. What's important to understand is that you've conflated two points together. Those two points are forgiveness and judgment. You can fully forgive someone, while at the same time know that any judgment they have coming will still take place. These are related points, but it's important to keep them separate in this discussion.

I have spoken many times about the power of forgiveness, and how important it is for men to forgive not only those who have hurt them, but also to forgive themselves, and let's come back to that point later. Clearly, I want people to forgive. It's a critical part of life for everyone.

I have also spoken about the fact that judgment is coming for all men. There's an ultimate and eternal judgment coming. However, notice that I never spoke of judgment coming only for "some people". It's coming for all, meaning you and both those who you have forgiven and those who you haven't forgiven.

In other words, I've said that every man will be judged, and I've said that every man is to forgive those who have done him wrong. In those two concepts, I do not say that forgiveness, in any way, will absolve someone of judgment.

You can fully forgive someone while knowing that the same someone will receive their ultimate justice.

With that in mind, don't get caught up, personally, on the judgment and justice side. That's where many men get tripped up and can often get hypocritical. Our Father in heaven is a good Father, and his ultimate justice will be final. It's your job, and that of every man, to focus on the forgiveness side.

Scriptures:

Matthew 18:21-22 "Then Peter came to him and asked, "Lord, how often should I forgive someone who sins against me? Seven times?" "No, not seven times, "Jesus replied, "but seventy times seven!"

Matthew 25:45-46 "And He will answer, "I tell you the truth, when you refused to help the least of these my brothers and sisters, you were refusing to help me. And they will go away into eternal punishment, but the righteous will go into eternal life."

Questions: Have you been holding back forgiveness, because you felt like you would be saying that what they did was ok? Who do you need to forgive, in your life?

FORGIVING YOURSELF

You said you wanted to come back to the idea of forgiving yourself later. How about we just follow-up and go right into that now? The idea of forgiving myself is very hard for me. I know I have made mistakes, mistakes that have hurt other people, or that have caused pain, and I continue to feel guilty about those mistakes. I guess I don't have a specific question, just want to hear what you have to say about the idea of forgiving yourself.

Jesus: I think for many men it's easier for them to forgive others than it is to forgive themselves. Men often feel that they can forgive someone else, as a benefit to that other person, while at the same time feel that it would be selfish to forgive themselves.

Forgiving yourself isn't selfish, just as loving yourself isn't selfish. Love is the cornerstone underneath forgiveness, and you've been given the command to love your neighbor as yourself. Notice that I said love your neighbor as yourself, I didn't say to love your neighbor and then sometime yourself. You are to love others in the same way as you are to love yourself.

Guilt, on the other hand, is different. To feel guilt after doing something wrong is perfectly understandable; it's part of how you know when you've sinned. However, never letting go of the guilt, not forgiving yourself, and not shifting your mind towards me is where the trouble comes in.

The repeated feeling of guilt is one that the enemy uses against you. You make a mistake, feel guilty about it, do not forgive yourself, relive the mistake in your mind, feel guilty again, and the cycle repeats. This attack is from the enemy and feeds the lie that you are to continue to feel guilty and should, therefore, continue to act guilty.

Holding onto guilt is a targeted attack so that you do not grow, learn, and become more. It's a trap to keep you stuck in that mental state. The enemy uses guilt to stop you from focusing your mind on me and the Father, to keep you from creating a stronger relationship with me, and to prevent you from studying the Word. I want you to let go of the guilt through forgiveness.

And always remember that loving yourself and forgiving yourself are directly connected, and neither is selfish. It's time for you to forgive, to love, and to thank the Father.

Scriptures:

Matthew 22:39 "A second is equally important: 'Love your neighbor as yourself.'"

Psalm 32:3 "When I refused to confess my sin, my body wasted away, and I groaned all day long."

Philippians 4:8 "And now, dear brothers and sisters, one final thing. Fix your thoughts on what is true, and honorable, and right, and pure, and lovely, and admirable. Think about things that are excellent and worthy of praise."

Questions: What areas of life do you still need to forgive yourself on? Next time, how will you pull yourself out of the cycle of guilt, which keeps you from fixing your thoughts on Jesus?

HAVE IT ALL

One thing I find sad is when I learn of a man who worked hard to "have it all", to maintain the image that he's living the perfect life, and then see this man's life crash down around him. He worked so hard to keep the image going, pushing harder and harder, while working longer and longer to keep up the façade. But when it inevitably crashes down, he ends up disillusioned and hurting people all around him. As common as this is, no one sets out for it to happen, so what are some warning signs a man can be on the lookout for?

Jesus: The worldly desire a man has for more, to appear to have everything together and to seem like he has it all together is strong. Men feel the pressure, often from their own peers, to seem like they have no problems and have more than their neighbors. Men also feel like the more wealth and material goods they surround themselves with, the happier they will be.

However, eventually, they realize that all the time focused on their own achievements, and the collection of more stuff in their lives, doesn't increase their contentment nor increase their happiness. These men end up feeling stuck, as their egos will not allow them to let go of their desire to have it all figured out.

One of the biggest warning signs is the loss of connection to anyone or anything that doesn't immediately return a worldly benefit back to them. When all conversations and interactions are based around a business, monetary, or image gain, that's a sign that a man is on this path.

The reality is that living for the world, or the approval of the world, will never bring contentment. And, the reality is that no man knows when his last day here on earth will be.

The life a man leads is not measured by his stuff, it's not measured by his house, and it's not measured by his bank account. On his last day, none of that will go with him.

If you're starting to feel that way, be willing to come to me with the challenge. Allow your old ways to wither and instead understand the peace and contentment of walking through life with me by your side. Allow yourself to experience the new life that I offer you.

Scriptures:

2 Corinthians 5:16-17 "So we have stopped evaluating others from a human point of view. At one time we thought of Christ merely from a human point of view. How differently we know him now! This means that anyone who belongs to Christ has become a new person. The old life is gone; a new life has begun!"

Philippians 4:12-13 "I know how to live on almost nothing or with everything. I have learned the secret of living in every situation, whether it is with a full stomach or empty, with plenty or little. For I can do everything through Christ, who gives me strength."

Luke 12:15 "Then he (Jesus) said, 'Beware! Guard against every kind of greed. Life is not measured by how much you own.'"

Questions: Have you ever felt yourself slipping into the trap of pursuing more, in order to have it all? What are you willing to let go of, in that pursuit, in order to escape the trap and live a more content life?

EVIL MONEY

We often hear about how money, or the lack of money, is at the source of so many problems in our world. We hear of men using their financial empires to control others, to manipulate others, and to only be concerned with their own self-interest. I think every man has plenty of thoughts about money, but what are your thoughts on the nature of money? Is money evil?

Jesus: Money is part of life here on earth, there's no way around it. People need some system of value to use in the exchange of goods and services, so I have no problem with money itself. I just want to get that point out of the way first.

What I do have a problem with is when men seek to become rich, above all their other desires including above their desire for a relationship with, and to know, me and the Father. When money moves to the top of their list of desires, it becomes an idol that they are seeking and inevitably end up serving. Such men can quickly become consumed with the pursuit of more money, trapped in an enslavement that they have unknowingly created for themselves.

Money is neither good nor evil; it's only a tool; no different than a hammer, chisel, or saw. Just as you cannot build a house without the hammer and saw, you cannot acquire the necessary materials without money; they're all tools to accomplish a task.

To your other question, a problem is indeed when people equate money with either good or evil, that is an improper equation. I hear some in your culture claiming that "money is the root of all evil" yet that's an incorrect citation. It's the "love of money" that is the problem. When money is loved, that's when trouble comes. When a man loves money, he is loving a false idol.

The truth is that a man cannot love money and seek to expand his relationship with me at the same time. He will end up focused on only one of those, and when he is consumed by earning money, he will not be deepening his connection with the Father.

Scriptures:

1 Timothy 6:9-10 "But people who long to be rich fall into temptation and are trapped by many foolish and harmful desires that plunge them into ruin and destruction. For the love of money is the root of all kinds of evil. And some people, craving money, have wandered from the true faith and pierced themselves with many sorrows."

Matthew 6:24 "No one can serve two masters. For you will hate one and love the other; you will be devoted to one and despise the other. You cannot serve God and be enslaved to money."

Questions: How badly do you want more money in your life? Has your desire for more money ever clouded your ability to remain connected with Jesus? Have you ever noticed that you cannot be solely focused on two things at once?

FAITH IN THE DARKNESS

*There have been times of serious darkness and trials in my life.
There were many times when I would rather have not woken up in
the morning. I know many other men have been in that same place
of darkness or are even there right now as they read this. How
should a man deal with the dark times and trials that this life so
often has?*

Jesus: The trials of life are a reality of life, there is no way around
that. The expectation that there won't be trials, or that if a man is a
follower of mine that he is somehow going to avoid trials is
unrealistic. Even I faced trials and temptation in my own life;
they're part of being alive.

The key to not only surviving but growing through the trials is faith.
Faith in what I've taught and faith in God the Father. Faith in your
modern culture is often thought of as simply accepting something
that cannot be scientifically proven, yet that isn't faith.

Faith is believing the word of God is true and acting accordingly.
Faith comes to a man who hears the good news I have come to
share and studies the Bible. Faith comes to a man who is willing to
set aside his pride, to listen, and to learn. Faith comes to a man who
is open-minded enough to allow me into his life so that I can be
there for him during the trials.

Two men may experience the exact same darkness and walk
through the exact same trials. The one who has faith and follows
me will be praised and honored as he moves into the light. Yet, the
man who has no faith and who does not follow me will struggle and
continue to experience the darkness.

So, for the man who is going through the dark times right now, the man who is facing the trial right now, come to me. Have faith in what I have taught. Have faith in what I have to teach. Pray for wisdom and insight. Read the word of God. Believe in the truth of God, your Father.

For you, there is light, there is joy, there is freedom, there is hope, and there is possibility. All of that comes with your faith. Have faith in the darkness, and you will see the light.

Scriptures:

1 Peter 1:6-7 "So be truly glad. There is wonderful joy ahead, even though you must endure many trials for a little while. These trials will show that your faith is genuine. It is being tested as fire tests and purifies gold – though your faith is far more precious than mere gold. So when your faith remains strong through many trials, it will bring you much praise and glory and honor on the day when Jesus Christ is revelated to the whole world."

Romans 5:1 "Therefore, since we have been made right in God's sight by faith, we have peace with God because of what Jesus Christ our Lord has done for us."

Questions: How often do you remember and think about the fact that Jesus faced trials and temptation in his life? What steps are you taking to deepen your faith?

DEPRESSION

One thing I never understood, until I experienced it myself, was what depression is really like. And when I did, it was unlike anything I expected, the darkness unlike anything else. In talking with lots of men, I know that many suffer quietly with this, trying to work everything out on their own. Did you ever deal with depression? What advice do you have for a man who is experiencing depression?

Jesus: Since the word depression has different meanings to different people, let me start by sharing this with you: Before I came, the prophet Isaiah wrote that I would be despised and that I would be rejected. He wrote that I would be a man of sorrows and that I would be acquainted with the deepest grief.

I certainly understood what that deepest kind of grief was like, having experienced it personally. One time, when I was suffering greatly, I even prayed to the Father that he would take away my suffering if it was His will, as the suffering was so severe.

I think men tend to push back with depression because they think it's somehow a form of weakness, or evidence of their failures. I can say with one-hundred percent assurance; it's not. No one experiences depression because they are weak.

Some of the strongest and most powerful men to ever walk on Earth have dealt with depression. The prophet Elijah got so beaten down he prayed for his life to be taken from him. King David was a powerful man, yet he openly shared his struggles with depression. Many other great men have done the same.

I would encourage all men to come to me when they are feeling that darkness, as I have experienced that same place and I understand. Pray to our Father, just as I did when I was suffering. Do not carry the burden alone, let me carry it for you.

And lastly, be strengthened by knowing so many great and powerful men before you have experienced depression as well. You're not alone. Be reassured by knowing that there is always light and that I'm always here for you.

Scripture:

Isaiah 53:3 "He was despised and rejected – a man of sorrows, acquainted with the deepest grief. We turned our backs on him and looked the other way. He was despised, and we did not care."

Luke 22:41-43 "He walked away, about a stone's throw, and knelt down and prayed, "Father, if you are willing, please take this cup of suffering away from me. Yet I want your will to be done, not mine." Then, an angel from heaven appeared and strengthened Him."

Hebrews 4:16 "So let us come boldly to the throne of our gracious God. There we will receive His mercy, and we will find grace to help us when we need it most."

Questions: Have you ever considered that Jesus may have experienced that darkness and grief himself? In your times of suffering, are you willing to pray to God, for His mercy and to receive His grace?

BREAKING POINT

In an interview, I was once asked which man in the Bible I could most relate with. Though it is different today, at that time my answer was Job. Having lost so much myself, I understood what he was going through. Hitting that breaking point is tough; when you realize life isn't about you and you no longer have all the answers. How do you help a man who is hitting his breaking point right now?

Jesus: When a man hits his breaking point, it's a very unique time in his growth, his development, and his life. Those moments are important in who the man is going to become, and while he doesn't know the outcome, he can choose the correct path to walk.

Two men may experience the exact same circumstance; they may be going through nearly identical breaking points, at the exact same time. The man who knows me, who has faith in me, and who is able to express gratitude for his life (even in the situation he currently finds himself in), will experience an entirely different outcome from the man who does not know me and who only relies on himself. It's the same breaking point for both men, but with very different outcomes.

One key is to understand that recovery from the breaking point will not come through logic, but rather it will come through trust. Emerging stronger on the other side will not come through strategy, but rather it will come through faith. Trust and Faith. Those are two cornerstones for a man going through a breaking point. He must maintain focus on his trust and faith in me.

Another key is to understand what Job realized, which was that God is not only Lord and present during the good times of life, but that he is Lord and present during the bad times as well. A man is not to accept only good things from God while refusing to accept the bad.

Lastly, is to remember that I'm always with you and that the Father is always with you. No matter the situation you find yourself in, I'm there. That doesn't mean you will always get the outcome that you personally want, but it does mean that you will never be abandoned or alone during those times. Your breaking point is an opportunity for you to become stronger than before.

Scriptures:

James 1:2-4 "Dear brothers and sisters, when troubles of any kind come your way, consider it an opportunity for great joy. For you know that when your faith is tested, your endurance has a chance to grow."

2 Chronicles 15:7 "But as for you, be strong and courageous, for your work will be rewarded."

Deuteronomy 31:8 "Do not be afraid or discouraged, for the Lord will personally go ahead of you. He will be with you; He will neither fail you nor abandon you."

Job 2:10 "But Job replied, 'You talk like a foolish woman. Should we accept only the good things from the hand of God and never anything bad?' So in all this, Job said nothing wrong."

Questions: When you hit your breaking point, do you consider that an opportunity for great joy? Do you remember that even during your most difficult times, that Lord is with you?

WORRY

When I look at the state of the world, it can seem scary. From the state of politics, to natural disasters, to disease, to the threat of war, there is lots to be concerned with. What do you say to a man who stays up at night thinking about these things and how they are risks to him and his family?

Jesus: I know times of uncertainty. My fishermen brothers would sometimes go fishing without bringing home any food to eat for their families. Communities, where I grew up, would deal with the reality that a severe drought could destroy an entire year's crops, leaving little to survive on through the winter. My very life was threatened by many leaders of the day. There was constantly something that I could have been worried about.

However, that worry would not have solved anything. That worry would not have advanced my purpose. That worry would not have added even one single day to my life.

To the man who is concerned by the risks of life, he is to recognize that worrying will never add anything positive to his life. Worrying cannot add another hour to the day, it cannot add any more money to a bank account, it cannot add another shirt to a closet, and it cannot add food to a homeless shelter.

Whenever something is a concern, whenever something is causing you to worry, bring that concern to the Father. During those times, focus first on the Father's kingdom and his great love for you. When you sense that worry is starting to slip into your thoughts, replace those thoughts with prayers of gratitude.

Always remember that there is nothing that will separate you from God's love, and that's an incredibly powerful reminder to keep with you throughout your days. No matter the situation you find yourself in, God's love for you continues. No matter the concerns of the day, God's love for you continues. Take solace in knowing this truth.

You are loved by God, every minute of every day.

Scriptures:

Matthew 6:27 "Can all your worries add a single moment to your life?"

Romans 8: 38-39 "And I am convinced that nothing can ever separate us from God's love. Neither death nor life, neither angels nor demons, neither our fears for today nor our worries about tomorrow – not even the powers of hell can separate us from God's love. No power in the sky above or in the earth below – indeed, nothing in all creation will ever be able to separate us from the love of God that is revealed in Christ Jesus our Lord."

Questions: How often do you find yourself worrying? Have you realized that worrying will never add another minute to your life? When you find yourself worrying, do you pray and give those worries to the Father?

POWER

Power is an interesting topic for men, and I think it will come up several times, in different ways, in our conversation. Watching the news any night and we can see examples of powerful men doing great things and also doing horrible things. I feel like it is man's nature to be drawn towards power, and that can't just be turned off. So, how should men think about the pursuit of power?

Jesus: The world can often have a strong pull on men, and one of the worldly things that draws men in is power. The desire for power to achieve, to create, to build, and even the desire for power over others is very strong in many men.

Men using their power to do great work, and to create amazing things, is a wonderful use of power. Modern technology and advances have connected the planet in wonderful ways and have extended lifespans in equally wonderful ways.

However, men pursuing power for the sake of power, or seeking power in order to control other people is a misuse of power and not the kind of power men should be pursuing. Instead, there is another power that I would prefer more men sought after. That's the power found in knowing me.

There's great inner strength in knowing me. There's great power in knowing me. My love for all men is truly limitless, which makes it impossible for you to comprehend truly. But my love for all men is greater than any object you could ever measure, including the universe itself. It's that vast.

In knowing me, men can fully transform themselves, which is a power unlike any other. Too often, when life gets hard, men pray for situations to change, but a situational change is always temporary. My own prayer is for people to change, because a man who changes his heart, who changes his love for others, and who seeks to understand me, is a powerful man who can have a profound and positive impact on this world. A man who knows me and uses that kind of power can perform miracles and can truly change everything.

Scripture:

Ephesians 3:16-19 "I pray that from his glorious, unlimited resources he will empower you with inner strength through his Spirit. Then Christ will make his home in your hearts as you trust in him. Your roots will grow down into God's love and keep you strong. And may you have the power to understand, as all God's people should, how wide, how long, how high, and how deep his love is. May you experience the love of Christ, though it is too great to understand fully. Then you will be made complete with all the fullness of life and power that comes from God."

Acts 6:8 "Stephen, a man full of God's grace and power, performed amazing miracles and signs among the people."

Questions: What kind of power are you seeking, in your life? Are you seeking the power of the world, or are you seeking the power to understand Jesus better?

GOD, THE FATHER

Sadly, too many men I know have not had great fathers, have had abusive fathers, or have never even met their fathers. That makes it difficult for them to know God as Father, or to know God as a good and loving Father. What do you say to such men?

Jesus: It breaks my heart when I see any suffering, or when I see any man who experiences such pain. Sons who have an earthly father who doesn't fulfill his duties isn't easy. Sons who have an earthly father who mistreats, abuses, or does not love his own children is a painful reality of this world.

Earthly fathers will have failings, as all men do. Earthly fathers will make mistakes, as all men do. Even the best men, who are trying hard to be the best fathers they can be, will make mistakes and fall down.

However, God the Father is unlike all earthly fathers, and cannot be compared to earthly fathers. God the Father will not make mistakes. God the Father will not fall down. God the Father will never leave you.

God the Father loves every man, period. With no exceptions. His love for every man is infinite, period. With no exceptions. God the Father loves you immeasurably. With no exceptions.

Your Father, in heaven, knew you before you were born. And not only did the Father know you before you were born, but the Father loved you before you were born.

God loves his creation, from the smallest animals to all of mankind. And since mankind is the most valuable of all his creation, His love for every man and woman is incalculable. Every man is called to love the Father, no matter the situation he was raised in.

In fact, even for those men blessed with incredible fathers, they're still called to love God the Father more. As wonderful as a great father is, it's even more important to build a relationship with and to love, God the Father, who loves you.

Every man must know that he has a good Father who loves him, a good Father who knows him, and a good Father who is always with him.

Scriptures:

Matthew 6:26 "Look at the birds. They don't plant or harvest or store food in barns, for your heavenly Father feeds them. And aren't you far more valuable to him than they are?"

John 17:24 "Father, I want these whom you have given me to be with me where I am. Then they can see all the glory you gave me because you loved me even before the world began!"

1 John 4:9 "God showed how much he loved us by sending his one and only Son into the world so that we might have eternal life through him."

Questions: Are you able to view God the Father as a good father who loves you? Are you ready to stop comparing earthly fathers with God the Father?

FATHER'S JOB

It's tough being a father. There are so many conflicting pressures on dads, as we juggle trying to be a good dad with our careers, our marriages, our finances, our health, and oh yeah, we're responsible for helping to shape our children into the adults they will become. With all that going on, how should us fathers set our priorities and what is one of the things that all fathers must make sure they do, or do first, as fathers?

Jesus: If everyone only had one thing to do in life, it would be easier - that's true. But it sure would be a boring, uninspiring, and dull life! All the intricacies of life are what gives it character, interest, and are where people can choose great happiness. Within the complexities of life is often where you can find the most beauty, and where you find the light within the darkness.

In all that complexity, as a father, you need to remain focused on your main job. That main job is for you to raise your children so that they know the Father, and that they know me and my teaching. That is more important than raising them to get into a specific school, or to excel at a specific sport, or to end up in a specific career.

In your culture of today, the emphasis is all about raising children to attend a specific college, but nowhere is that part of my teaching. Children today are often told that they're to attend and participate in event after event, but again that's nowhere in my teaching.

When a father focuses all his time and energy on leading his children towards earthly goals, such as pushing a son or daughter to excel at a specific sport, that father should not be surprised when his child becomes frustrated, aggravated, or even angry. Children need fathers who are respectful, and who are understanding of who they are becoming as they grow up.

Fathers might have good intentions in pushing their kids in such ways, but such intentions only cloud the desire for a relationship with me. A father's job, his main priority, is to teach his children about me and lead them onto the path towards the Father's kingdom.

Scriptures:

Ephesians 6:4 "Fathers, do not provoke your children to anger by the way you treat them. Rather, bring them up with the discipline and instruction that comes from the Lord."

Colossians 3:21 "Fathers, do not aggravate your children, or they will become discouraged."

Proverbs 22:6 "Direct your children onto the right path, and when they are older, they will not leave it."

Questions: Are you pushing your children to a specific school or sport, more than you are teaching them about the way of Jesus? What would be different in your family if you changed what you are teaching your children about with a focus towards Jesus?

ESTRANGED SON

A man I know is facing great challenges with one of his sons. This son has done bad things, he has turned his back on his parents, and he has abandoned the values he was raised with. He holds different political views from his father and uses that against his father. This man has not seen, or spoken to, his son in years, and I know he is in great pain from this. What should this man do, if or when he finally does see his son again?

Jesus: These are always painful stories. Children and parents should never be willfully apart in this manner. I'm always saddened when family members choose to be estranged from one another. That should never happen, especially over something of the world such as politics.

The rebellion of children is common and is part of human free will. The father here has only two main choices. His first choice is to become bitter, angry, and resentful of what his son has done. His second choice is to pray for his son, wait for or attempt to arrange his return, and prepare to bless him when he comes home.

I would tell this father that he is to show mercy, grace, and love to his son. That when he does see his son again, he is to run to his child and embrace him fully.

When lost children return home, it's a joyous occasion, one that calls for a celebration, not a lecture or a speech. The son already feels guilt as he knows that he has caused pain and has made bad decisions, there's no benefit in reliving those moments during the reunion.

This man is to joyously embrace the return of his son, just as the Father in heaven will with you.

Every man on earth, including you, will make some mistake that will move him further away from the Father, yet the Father is still waiting for you with open arms. And when you do return home to the Father, he will joyously embrace you and celebrate that you are with him. You are to show the same love for your children coming home to you as the Father will when you come home to him.

Scriptures:

Luke 15:20-24 "So he returned home to his father. And while he was still a long way off, his father saw him coming. Filled with love and compassion, he ran to his son, embraced him, and kissed him. His son said to him, 'Father, I have sinned against both heaven and you, and I am no longer worthy of being called your son.' But his father said to the servants, 'Quick! Bring the finest robe in the house and put it on him. Get a ring for his finger and sandals for his feet. And kill the calf we have been fattening. We must celebrate with a feast, for this son of mine was dead and now has returned to life. He was lost, but now he is found.' So the party began."

Questions: Have you turned away from what Jesus has taught you? Are you ready to return home, to God?

DISCIPLINE DAD

I usually know when I've made a mistake, as a father, by how my kids react. I know if I said something too strongly, or if I looked at one of my kids the wrong way. I know because I can feel it in my heart and in how they respond. What's the right way to discipline my children?

Jesus: Being a father certainly is a job with many challenges, but it's also one of the most important jobs any man could ever have. Raising up your sons and daughters to become faith-filled, loving, and good adults is as daunting a task as any a man can take on.

Too often a father will focus only on discipline, excelling in sports or other activities, or getting good grades in their schooling. A father who ends up putting too much pressure on his children, or only being the disciplinarian of the house, can cause a divide between himself and his kids. And when that pressure continues, the divide can turn the child towards anger, resentment, and the choice to walk down a separate path in life. Some children will make their aggravation and anger clearly known, while others will hold it inside until they can no longer, and neither of those is a good situation.

Don't look at discipline as a means of punishing bad behavior. Instead, look at discipline as a means of training. Earlier I spoke about your training, and the discipline required in your training. Consider the discipline of your children in the same manner, a way for them to learn how to stay on the right path.

When you must discipline to correct behavior, do so with love. Do so with the intention of teaching. Do so with the desire that your relationship together grows stronger. Do so with the well-being of their hearts in mind.

Because you must always guard the hearts of your children. They are going to be influenced by the world at every turn, so they need to know that you have their backs, and they need to be raised to know me. Your children are to be taught about me and about the Father.

You are to model for them what it looks like to experience a loving relationship with me. You are to set the example for them about how to live their own lives as someone who is not of this world. That's the discipline you should focus on.

Scriptures:

Colossians 3:21 "Fathers, do not aggravate your children, or they will become discouraged."

Ephesians 6:4 Fathers, do not provoke your children to anger by the way you treat them. Rather, bring them up with the discipline and instruction that comes from the Lord."

Proverbs 22:6 "Direct your children onto the right path, and when they are older, they will not leave it."

2 Timothy 3:15 "You have been taught the holy Scriptures from childhood, and they have given you the wisdom to receive the salvation that comes by trusting in Christ Jesus."

Questions: How can you show your children love, while at the same time correcting poor behavior or choices? How can you model a relationship with Jesus, as a man who knows that you make your own mistakes?

BREAK THE CHAIN

Most men end up like their fathers, for both good and bad. Even men who never met their own fathers often end up eerily like their absent fathers. Sometimes this is used as an excuse for poor behavior, with guys saying things like, "Well, that's how my dad was." When we know there is something that we do not want to pass down to our own children, how do we break that cycle?

Jesus: There are generational chains that men have to deal with, for sure. Sons are like their fathers, who are like their fathers, who are like their fathers, and on and on. Sometimes a family or character trait can easily be traced back many generations.

When a father is abusive, often times his father was abusive to him. When a father is an alcoholic, often times his father was an alcoholic. Those truths cannot be used as excuses, as each man is held accountable for his own choices and his own actions. Rather they are examples of chains that must be intentionally be broken.

The beginning of breaking the chain is for each man to be determined and committed to doing so. Meaning each man must make the conscious choice of what character trait he is going to break and refuse to pass down to his own children. When every man breaks one or two links on the chain, for every generation, it's not long until the negative character traits of the past are no longer in the present.

When the chain isn't broken, then the child will end up dealing with the same repercussions as the father. When the father was punished, be it here on earth or in the afterlife, for what he had done wrong, and if that same wrong is passed down to his son, when the son commits the same wrong, the son will likewise deal with similar consequences.

On the other hand, when a son makes the conscious choice to live a different life, to not follow down those negative footsteps, he will be on the path to a new life and will be setting up future generations on that positive path.

Scriptures:

Lamentations 5:7 "Our ancestors sinned, but they have died – and we are suffering the punishment they deserved!"

Ezekiel 18:14, 17 "But suppose that sinful son, in turn, has a son who sees his father's wickedness and decides against that kind of life. Such a person will not die because of his father's sins; he will surely live."

Questions: What link, in your family chain, were you given by your father, that you are determined to break? What negative trait are you consciously working on to make sure it is not passed down to your children? What positive trait are you intentionally making sure you do pass to the next generation?

HEALING THE FATHER WOUND

Earlier I mentioned how many men I know have had very poor relationships with their fathers or have never known their fathers. I also know plenty of other men who have had nice and kind fathers, but who were mostly absent as the men walked through their challenges in life. This father wound is complex, and not the same for every man, so how should a man go about healing it?

Jesus: One of the primary roles of a father is to bring out the positive masculine nature of his son. When the father doesn't do this, or when he gives the responsibility to a boy's mother, this wound can begin. There are other forms of the father wound, but I'm going to focus on this one right now.

What often happens then is the boy grows up to become an adult, but he still hasn't been taught how to be a man. It's a mistake to think this happens automatically, as it does not. Manhood is bestowed from a father to a son; it's not automatic. When it doesn't happen, then those adult men look towards popular culture or try to heal their wound themselves.

However, no man can heal his own wound. No matter how much he may want to do good, or how much he may want to improve, when he looks to himself, or to other men with similar wounds, there will be no healing found.

Healing of this wound comes through a relationship with me, and with your heavenly Father. Healing comes when you accept that this wound exists (it's a great lie of your enemy to make you think you're exempt from this wound), and when you acknowledge that you can't heal yourself. Healing comes when you let go and allow me to perform the healing.

There's no shame in this acknowledgment, no embarrassment in this reality, and no guilt in this understanding. There's only power, growth, peace, and contentment.

It's my job to walk you through healing this wound, so let me. It's the Fathers job to welcome you to the place that has already been prepared for you, so let him. We're ready for you to ask.

Scriptures:

Romans 7:18-19 "And I know that nothing good lives in me, that is, in my sinful nature. I want to do what is right, but I can't. I want to do what is good, but I don't. I don't want to do what is wrong, but I do it anyway."

Psalm 27:10 "Even if my father and mother abandon me, the Lord will hold me close."

1 Peter 2:24 "He personally carried our sins so that we can be dead to sin and live for what is right. By his wounds you are healed."

Psalm 23:3-4 "He renews my strength. He guides me along right paths, bringing honor to his name. Even when I walk through the darkest valley, I will not be afraid, for you are close beside me. Your rod and your staff protect and comfort me."

Questions: What father wound are you struggling with? Are you ready to acknowledge that the wound exists, and willing to ask Jesus to heal that wound?

LEGACY

As men get a bit older, as they have children of their own, and as they become grandfathers, the idea of legacy becomes more significant. There is less focus on achieving for themselves, and more focus on the future, beyond them. What does it mean for a man to build a legacy that he leaves for his family?

Jesus: There is more than one kind of legacy that a man can leave when he's no longer living on earth. The most obvious answer is a financial legacy, which is why that's what men tend to focus on. There's nothing wrong with you earning enough money (keeping our conversation about money in mind here) and financial wealth to pass that along to the generations that follow you.

However, that's not the only kind of legacy to leave, nor is it even the most important kind, which tends to surprise most men. Much more important than your financial or material legacy is the spiritual legacy you leave behind. It's your job to lead those around you, to show them your love of the Father, and to teach them what your faith means.

A man may have little to leave his family, in terms of material goods, but he may leave a positive spiritual legacy that will last for generations. On the other hand, a man may leave his family much, in terms of material goods, but if he has not left his family a spiritual legacy, he may be forgotten quickly.

Once a man becomes aware of the fact that he will leave a legacy, it is his job to intentionally work on building his legacy. Because a father will pass on his legacy, whether he realizes it or not.

His legacy is being built, every day. A man's actions are noticed by his children, his wife, and his community, and those actions are all part of his legacy. Men need to become active in this process and build the legacy that brings glory to the Father's kingdom. That's the kind of legacy that truly lasts generations.

Scriptures:

Deuteronomy 6:5-7 "And you must love the Lord your God with all your heart, all your soul, and all your strength. And you must commit yourselves wholeheartedly to these commands that I am giving you today. Repeat them again and again to your children, when you are going to bed and when you are getting up."

Proverbs 13:22 "Good people leave an inheritance to their grandchildren, but the sinner's wealth passes to the godly."

Questions: Are you more interested in leaving a financial legacy than a spiritual one? Are you actively working on building both types of legacies for your children and grandchildren? How are you building your spiritual legacy?

POTENTIAL

Sometimes I get upset because I feel like I'm not living up to my full potential. I feel like I could be doing so much more, but I'm not. I feel like I'm busy, but not really doing the things I should be doing. How do I make sure that I am fulfilling my potential?

Jesus: Men often will fall into the trap of feeling like they have to do more and more, that they have to continue to acquire and accomplish more and more. Men think that the accomplishments are tired to potential. However, this is a trap that ultimately leads to being unsettled and upset, because the "more" that men are after is a moving target, one that always continues to move farther away.

Every time a man achieves something, or hits a certain level of income, or acquires a new business, he notices a brand-new target that's just a bit farther down the road. So, he sets his sights on that new target, achieves it, and remains unsettled in his inner self.

The reality is that none of that achieving, as the world sees it, matters to me. And that's why the empty feeling is still there inside when a man reaches a new goal. Instead of seeking a deeper relationship with me, and seeking to understand the Father better, he is seeking more of this world. As he continues to seek more of this world, his feeling of emptiness never goes away, even as he continues to pursue more and more.

When he makes, and when you make, the shift towards following me, towards knowing me better, towards understanding the Father more, suddenly that internal struggle with potential dissolves. Living up to your potential is found in the Father and in me.

A man is required to love his neighbors, to do what is right, to be merciful, to extend grace, and to humbly walk before God the Father. Doing that every day is living up to your potential.

And then, beyond doing that yourself, teaching others about me is taking it up to the next level. Take what you have learned about me, about the Father, about the Holy Spirit, and spread that good news with everyone on Earth. Do this, and you will experience an inner peace to go along with the understanding that you are living up to your heavenly potential.

Scriptures:

Micah 6:8 "No, O people, the Lord has told you what is good, and this is what he requires of you: to do what is right, to love mercy, and to walk humbly with your God."

Matthew 28:18-20 "Jesus came and told his disciples, 'I have been given all authority in heaven and on earth. Therefore, go and make disciples of all the nations, baptizing them in the name of the Father and the Son and the Holy Spirit. Teach these new disciples to obey all the commands I have given you. And be sure of this: I am with you always, even to the end of the age.'"

Questions: Do you measure your potential by the ways of the world, or by how Jesus measures it? Are you sharing the good news of Jesus with everyone you can?

POLITICS

We live in strange times, politically speaking. Political parties and systems all claiming to have the answers, often brutally vilifying their opponents in the process. Throughout your time on earth, it seemed to me like you remained neutral on the issue of politics. Is that still the same today?

Jesus: I have never had any desire to be involved in any human political system. I certainly would never be part of any political party in any government. My desire is greater than local political conversations.

I had no desire to be a king here on Earth, and when some people thought I should, I removed myself from the situation and went to the hills to pray. I absolutely refused to get involved in politics then, and I will do the same today. Politics are of this world, and my desire for humanity is greater. The Father's kingdom, the kingdom I am part of, isn't found here on earth.

Humans have shown over thousands of years of history, in every form of government, that no matter how good their intentions may be, they cannot overcome the world itself. Humankind has an enemy that corrupts, and this enemy enjoys taking advantage of the power of political systems.

Political systems are required on Earth; there needs to be structure, a system in place to maintain order, and a means of upholding reasonable laws. While I understand that these systems are required, I will not put myself into those systems, as they are of this world.

My disciples were likewise not involved in politics. They had accepted my task of teaching the world about me and my purpose here on Earth. My disciples made the choice to worship the Father, and not become part of the political system, nor sit in any political office.

I am here to teach and lead all people to my Father's kingdom, no matter what earthly political system they might find themselves temporarily in. My desire is for all people, of all political systems, of all political parties, and on all continents to come to me and home to the Father.

Scriptures:

John 6:14-15 "When the people saw him do this miraculous sign, they exclaimed, 'Surely, he is the Prophet we have been expecting!' When Jesus saw that they were ready to force him to be their king, he slipped away into the hills by himself."

John 18:36 "Jesus answered, 'My Kingdom is not an earthly kingdom. If it were, my followers would fight to keep me from being handed over to the Jewish leaders. But my Kingdom is not of this world.'"

Questions: Have you ever tried to make Jesus fit into your own political beliefs? Have you ever considered that the reason political systems become corrupt is not due to any individual politician, but rather due to the enemy who corrupts people?

HATE

When I read books about you, they usually focus on the loving and kind side of you. I aspire to that; I want to be as kind and loving as I can myself. But there are times when the other parts of me come out as well. Can you relate to that? For example, did you ever hate anything?

Jesus: It's an interesting point you raise, as I'm aware that many refer to me as only loving and kind. And, if I could teach only one point, it would be for men to love the Father, to love their families, to love their neighbors, to love strangers, and even to love their enemies. Love and kindness certainly are located in the heart and foundation of every strong man.

With that being said, Yes. I can relate to what you're asking about. But hate can be a very dangerous thing and is something that men have to be extraordinarily careful with. Hate can easily open the door for the enemy to use in corrupting the man. Hate can quickly open the door to sin.

But the question shouldn't be about hate itself; rather it should be about what it is that receives your hate. If you have any hatred in your heart for a fellow human, that's not ok, it's a sin, and you need to pray for forgiveness and to remove that entirely from your heart. Hating another person, no matter how justified you may feel, requires you to repent.

If you have any concern about this, you should pray, right now, to the Father. Ask him to reveal your heart, confess any hatred for another person that you might be holding, ask for forgiveness, and ask him to show you a new way forward. Because it's never acceptable to hate another man.

On the other hand, hating evil is acceptable. And not only is it ok for you to hate evil, throughout the Word you can read time and time again that you are told to hate evil. You're actually instructed to hate evil.

Evil and sin destroy people, they destroy families, they destroy hope. Evil and sin lead to despair, they lead to corruption, and they lead to pain. Hating evil and hating sin is most certainly what a good man should do.

Men must be willing to stand up and confront evil and sin. Men must be willing to hate them both.

Scriptures:

Revelation 2:6 "But this is in your favor: You hate the evil deeds of the Nicolaitans, just as I do."

Psalm 97:10 "You who love the Lord, hate evil! He protects the lives of his godly people and rescues them from the power of the wicked."

Proverbs 13:5 "The godly hate lies; the wicked cause shame and disgrace."

Questions: Have you ever considered that Jesus hated evil? Had you noticed that the Bible calls you to hate evil, just as Jesus does?

COMPARISON

Our social media world has made it so a man can almost instantly compare his life to another man's. He can easily compare houses, cars, careers, families, and on and on. I admit that I've fallen into this myself sometimes. When I do that, I end up feeling bad about myself, even though I work hard to be grateful for all that I have been blessed with. How should we deal with the instant comparison world we live in?

Jesus: One man comparing his life to his neighbor's life has been going on for as long as written history. But the fact that it has been taking place for ages does not mean it's a positive thing. Comparison can lead to envy and can lead men to taking negative actions they would never otherwise take if they weren't comparing themselves to other men.

Even my own disciples, who were standing with me, were challenged with comparing themselves to one another. They wanted to know who would be seated by my side in heaven. So, you're in good company with this struggle. Many, if not all, men are challenged with comparisons during their lives.

The enemy uses your comparisons to make you feel inadequate, small, and unsuccessful. Those feelings lead to more negative thoughts, which can lead to negative actions.

Men who choose to pridefully make themselves superior, through their own words or in comparison to each other, are simply showing their ignorance of me, of the Father, and of the greater things in life.

The key is to shift from a position of comparison to a position of contentment and gratitude. Gratitude is a powerful antidote against comparison. And, when you're feeling the pull of comparison, use that as an opportunity instead to pray and strengthen your faith.

Be grateful for the life you do have, build your faith into an even stronger foundation, as these two things will help to counter the pull of comparison. And remember, the Father only made one of you, exactly as you are, and that you were wonderfully created by him.

Scriptures:

2 Corinthians 10:12 "Oh, don't worry; we wouldn't dare say that we are as wonderful as these other men who tell you how important they are! But they are only comparing themselves with each other, using themselves as the standard of measurement. How ignorant!"

Exodus 20:17 "You must not covet your neighbor's house. You must not covet your neighbor's wife, male or female servant, ox or donkey, or anything else that belongs to your neighbor."

Galatians 6:4 "Pay careful attention to your own work, for then you will get the satisfaction of a job well done, and you won't need to compare yourself to anyone else."

Questions: Where are you comparing yourself to other men? Do you find yourself wishing you have what other men have? Are you able to be content with a job well done or do you wish you had a more prestigious job?

LIVING DIFFERENTLY

When I see how some people act and talk, sometimes even in the parking lot on the way out from a church service, I can understand people who think that some Christians are often hypocrites. What is supposed to be different about a Christian man, other than attending a church service?

Jesus: The men who are my followers are to live a life that is different from the ways of the world. I want my followers to show and demonstrate such love for one another that people stop and notice. I want my followers to share my good news with the world. I want my followers to be living a life that demands an explanation.

If there's no difference between the men who are my followers and non-believers, then those who are claiming to know me, do not fully know me. I do expect that my followers will live a life that is different.

Those who truly know me can live a life of peace and contentment that the rest of the world cannot. Those who truly know me are to shine a light for everyone to see, they are to love one another in such a manner that others do notice something is different. Those who truly know me are to live such an honorable life that when someone tries to criticize them, those critics will be silenced, and their accusations will be deemed foolish.

The men who are my followers are not to be conformed to the ways of the world; rather they are to set a positive example for all, in every aspect of their lives. From the way that they think to the way that they act, there should be an obvious difference between my followers and non-believers.

It's not easy to live your life differently from the world; I fully understand that. However, it's worth it as it changes your entire life for the better. The Father notices every man who is living a life that is set apart from the world. He rejoices with every decision and action that is made to honor Him. And so do I!

Scriptures:

John 13:35 "Your love for one another will prove to the world that you are my disciples."

Romans 5:1-2 "Therefore, since we have been made right in God's sight by faith, we have peace with God because of what Jesus Christ our Lord has done for us. Because of our faith, Christ has brought us into this place of undeserved privilege where we now stand, and we confidently and joyfully look forward to sharing God's glory."

1 Peter 2:15 "It is God's will that your honorable lives should silence those ignorant people who make foolish accusations against you."

Titus 2:7-8 "Show yourself in all respects to be a model of good works, and in your teaching show integrity, dignity, and sound speech that cannot be condemned, so that an opponent may be put to shame, having nothing evil to say about us." (ESV)

Questions: Would someone know you are a follower of Jesus by how you speak, how you act, and how you live? Are you prepared to live differently, for him?

ACT LIKE A MAN

All over the world, it seems like men are in trouble, confused, or hurting. Men are silent about this, as they struggle to figure out who they should be, and how they should act. The world seems to be constantly sending mixed messages to men. I know I get exhausted just trying to keep up, so how should a man act?

Jesus: Although there never will be one single answer for how all men should act, there certainly are some common principles that are good for all men. Those principles, for how men should act, can all be found in the Scriptures and in the example that I set for men. If a man lives as I lived, he is acting as a man should.

One set of actions was written by Paul, instructing that men should be watchful, be strong, and stand firm in the faith. Those are all excellent, and I also want to point out that he added that a man is also to let all things be done in love. Underneath everything else, there must be a foundation of love.

Since this one question could take up our entire conversation, here are some quick points:

A man fights. He fights for what is right, and what is true. He knows that he is in a battle for his very soul, he puts on his armor, and he fights.

A man is a leader, a warrior, and a friend. As a leader, a man provides, as a warrior, he protects, and as a friend, he loves. Again, underneath everything else, there must be a foundation of love.

A man acts with humility. He knows that he doesn't have it all figured out and is at peace with the fact that he never will.

A man is not a boy. He learns, he gains wisdom, he matures, and he grows up.

A man seeks the Father and a relationship with me. He knows that through the gift of his life from the Father and through a relationship with me, he can become the man he was created to be. He knows he can act like a man, because he is one.

Scriptures:

1 Corinthians 16:13-14 "Be watchful, stand firm in the faith, act like men, be strong. Let all that you do be done in love." (ESV)

1 Timothy 6:12 "Fight the good fight for the true faith. Hold tightly to the eternal life to which God has called you, which you have declared so well before many witnesses."

1 Corinthians 13:11 "When I was a child, I spoke like a child, I thought like a child, I reasoned like a child. When I became a man, I gave up childish things." (ESV)

Questions: How do you think Jesus wants you to act, as a man? What traits of acting like a man, according to our culture, does Jesus want you to have? Which of those cultural traits does he not want you to have?

THE MASK

When I find myself in a new situation with other men, I sometimes feel like I have to pretend that I already know what they know. I want to fit it and be one of the guys. I don't want to appear like I'm the one guy who doesn't know what's going on. I'm worried they won't think well of me if they knew how little I knew about the stuff they know about. How do I learn to feel comfortable and honest in those situations?

Jesus: When you're concerned with what other men will think about what you say or do, you have transferred your power to them. When you're wondering how others will respond to you, you're not living in the freedom that you were created to live in.

When you live in the freedom that I offer, you are living boldly, with nothing to hide and nothing to fear. This type of freedom allows you to remove your masks, all of them. This type of freedom is unlike any other because it's life-giving no matter the situation you find yourself in.

If you're not living in this freedom, then you will continue to wear your masks, anxious about the response of the world to who you are, what you say, and how you act. Wearing the mask will cause you to stumble, to fall, and to find yourself saying and doing things that you know are not true to who you were created to be.

Even my disciple Peter wore a mask and fell this way. He was not willing to admit he knew me, to the point that he denied knowing me three times. This was a man who was by my side, who knew me well, and who knew my everlasting love for him. But, the pull of the world was strong, and his fear over being found out made him wear a mask of not knowing me.

As you become more comfortable living in my freedom, you will become more comfortable in those situations. Because, you will come to understand that it's not about the reaction of the other men in this world, rather it's about your relationship with me and the freedom that I offer you.

Scriptures:

2 Corinthians 3:17-18 "For the Lord is the Spirit, and wherever the Spirit of the Lord is, there is freedom. So all of us who have had that veil removed can see and reflect the glory of the Lord. And the Lord – who is the Spirit – makes us more and more like him as we are changed into his glorious image."

1 John 2:4 "If someone claims, 'I know God,' but doesn't obey God's commandments, that person is a lair and is not living in the truth."

Mark 14:66-68 "Meanwhile, Peter was in the courtyard below. One of the servant girls who worked for the high priest came by and noticed Peter warming himself at the fire. She looked at him closely and said, 'You were one of those with Jesus of Nazareth.' But Peter denied it. 'I don't know what you're talking about,' he said, and he went out into the entryway. Just then, a rooster crowed."

Questions: What masks are you currently wearing, that you know you have to remove? Do you have a man that you can be totally free and honest with, about anything in your life? If not, what steps will you take to build a relationship with a man to be that person for you?

LEADING

Almost every man I know wants to become a better leader. He wants to be a leader that is effective, and that people want to follow. However, even though most men want this, most men haven't been taught how to become a great leader. What should a man do to become a great leader?

Jesus: To become a great leader, either in his home, his community or in his career, a man must possess several characteristics. Some of these come more naturally than others, but all can be worked on, and all can be improved upon by every man.

First, a great leader is trustworthy. He follows through on his commitments, and he sets an example by refusing to break laws or rules in order to get ahead. He's a man of his word, and no matter if he's leading just a few people or is leading millions, people can count on him and trust him.

Second, a great leader is concerned about what's best for his followers. He doesn't do things for his own personal gain, or simply to raise his own standing. He genuinely cares about the things his followers care about, and he works towards creating solutions for all.

Third, a great leader is to be held accountable. He knows that his words and his actions will one day be judged and that he cannot escape such judgment. He knows that he will stand before the Father and be held to account for what he has done with his life.

A man who is trustworthy, who is concerned about his followers, and remembers that he will be held accountable is a man who is on the right path towards becoming a great leader.

As one last point, never forget that you may feel called to be a great leader, but you can never force anyone to follow you. You might focus on each of these characteristics, work hard at improving in them, but there will still be people who choose another path. Do not let that dishearten you. Continue to be a great leader and when those people return, welcome them with open arms.

Scriptures:

Exodus 18:21 "But select from all the people some capable, honest men who fear God and hate bribes. Appoint them as leaders over groups of one thousand, one hundred, fifty, and ten."

Numbers 27:16-17 "O Lord, you are the God who gives breath to all creatures. Please appoint a new man as leader for the community. Give them someone who will guide them wherever they go and will lead them into battle, so the community of the Lord will not be like sheep without a shepherd."

Hebrews 13:17 "Obey your spiritual leaders and do what they say. Their work is to watch over your souls, and they are accountable to God. Give them reason to do this with joy and not with sorrow."

Questions: What kind of leader are you trying to become? Are you a trustworthy leader? Are you a leader who is concerned about his followers? Are you a leader who is joyfully ready to be held to account?

SERVING

I think most men have had a bad boss at some time, and most men never want to become that bad boss themselves. So what's something a leader can do, directly for his followers, to make sure he doesn't become the bad boss that no one wants to follow?

Jesus: A great leader does not simply command others, telling them what to do and when to do it. A great leader is one who serves those he has been called to lead. A great leader is one who will humble himself and become a servant of his followers.

For many, this is a contradiction, as they wonder how can one be both a great leader and a servant at the same time? But what those men miss is that it's through the act of serving that a leader becomes truly great. A great leader is even willing and ready to die for those he is leading.

A great leader serves the Father first, and he does not lead in order to gain public acceptance, fame, or fortune. A great leader is filled with joy when he sees the success and happiness of the people he is leading. A great leader is happy to give up his own benefits for the gain of his followers. A great leader knows that his time of leadership will end, he looks forward to when it will end, and he gratefully builds up other leaders to carry the mantle when that time comes.

Beyond working to be a humble servant leader in your career, you are to follow this same idea for how you lead your family. You're called to serve your family in this same manner. You are to lead your family, by serving your family.

Lastly, do not misuse your position as a servant leader; doing so only shows that you have not yet grasped this idea. Don't serve, with the expectation that in doing so you will have followers. Serving others isn't a strategy for gaining followers, it's a directive in how to live your life as a leader. Remember that all leaders will be held accountable, before the Father, for their words and their actions.

Scriptures:

Matthew 6:25-26 "But Jesus called them together and said, 'You know that the rulers in this world lord it over their people, and officials flaunt their authority over those under them. But among you it will be different. Whoever wants to be a leader among you must be your servant."

Mark 10:45 "For even the Son of Man came not to be served but to serve others and to give his life as a ransom for many."

John 10:11 "I am the good shepherd. The good shepherd sacrifices his life for the sheep."

Questions: Where in your life are you currently a servant leader? Are you looking to lead in order to gain acceptance, fame, or fortune? Have you ever manipulated someone into following you? How are you a servant leader in your family?

MENTORING

I want to ask more about leadership. One of the areas of leadership we didn't get into is mentoring. Most men don't have mentors, and many are not even interested in having a mentor. What are your thoughts on men both having mentors and being mentors?

Jesus: One of the most important things a great leader needs to do is to create more great leaders by mentoring others. If you're responsible for leading others, but you're not mentoring those who follow you, you're missing out on a critical aspect of being that great leader. Mentoring is how your ideas, thoughts, and inspiration expands beyond yourself and flows to generations.

A wise man will seek out different mentors, for different areas of his life. A wise man will listen to his mentors. A wise man will learn from his mentors. A wise man will seek me to be his personal mentor. A wise man will learn from the Word.

When the idea of mentoring comes up, wise men understand how a mentor will benefit them, but they tend to miss the other side of the equation. Meaning, the focus should never be solely on finding someone to be your mentor but should also include who you are going to mentor. It's not a one-way street. Just as you need others to pour into your life, you need to pour into the lives of others.

With my disciples, I was mentoring them constantly. I was preparing them for the work they would be doing in the future. I was inspiring them with powerful truths. I was teaching them. I was correcting them. I was modeling behavior and language for them to emulate. I was showing them their potential.

In other words, I was mentoring them in all aspects of their lives. I knew that one day I would no longer walk the earth beside them and that they would carry on the mission. They were, after all, the first missionaries here and I needed to mentor them so that they would be equipped for that work.

As a mentor, you're instructed to do the same. You are to pour your own life, experience, and wisdom into those you will mentor so that one day they can go out into the world and carry the message. As a mentor, who shares my good news, you are fishing for men, exactly like my first disciples.

Scriptures:

Luke 24:32 "They said to each other, 'Didn't our hearts burn within us as he talked with us on the road, and explained the Scriptures to us?"

Luke 6:40 "Students are not greater than their teacher. But the student who is fully trained will become like the teacher."

John 20:21 "Again he said, 'Peace be with you. As the Father has sent me, so I am sending you."

Matthew 4:19 "And he said to them, 'Come, follow me, and I will make you fishers of men." (ESV)

Questions: Do you have mentors in your life, right now? If not, what are you doing to change that? Who are you mentoring right now? If no one, what are you doing to change that? How will you allow Jesus to be your personal mentor?

WORKING

I feel like the drive to work is inherent in men, that men were created to work. Sometimes it seems that isn't the case though, and there are plenty of men who simply choose not to work, relying on others instead. I'm not referring to men who cannot work, for whatever reason; I'm talking about those who choose not to work. Is a man supposed to work?

Jesus: Starting with Adam, who was given the first work assignment from the Father, men were created to work. As a man, your work is part of what motivates you and part of what defines you. The feeling of accomplishing hard work is a great feeling that all men should know and enjoy.

When you work hard, in your career, in your home, or anywhere you are working, you're accomplishing things. Your work is providing, which I'm sure we'll talk more about. Your work is allowing your family to have security. Your work is allowing your family to have safety.

Even when the work isn't what you would prefer to do, it's important for you to complete your work to the best of your ability. Not every man will work at his dream job, in fact, most men will never work at their dream jobs. However, that should not limit any man's enthusiasm or professionalism.

When you work hard, on a consistent basis, you're able to not only take care of yourself and your immediate family, but you're able to take care of others. A man who has nothing is not able to give to those in need, outside of his time and energy (which is obviously important). However, a man who has earned plenty, through his hard work, is able to give generously to many.

And, no matter what the job is, no matter what work you're doing, you should work as if you're working directly for the Father. You should work as if I'm standing by your side all day long, encouraging you to do your work well. Because, I am.

Scriptures:

Genesis 2:15 "The Lord God took the man and put him in the Garden of Eden to work it and take care of it."

Ephesians 4:28 "If you are a thief, quit stealing. Instead use your hands for good work, and then give generously to others in need."

2 Thessalonians 3:8,10 "We never accepted food from anyone without paying for it. We worked hard day and night so we would not be a burden to any of you. Even while we were with you, we gave you this command: 'Those unwilling to work will not get to eat.'"

Proverbs 28:19 "A hard worker has plenty of food, but a person who chases fantasies ends up in poverty."

1 Corinthians 15:58 "So, my dear brothers and sisters, be strong and immovable. Always work enthusiastically for the Lord, for you know that nothing you do for the Lord is ever useless."

Questions: Are you doing your work as if you are working for the Father? How would your work change, if you knew that Jesus was by your side, all day long as you worked?

YOU ARE THE TARGET

In my life, I often have to deal with not believing in myself enough. I think there are other people more capable, more competent, more effective, or simply more able to do the things I feel like I've been called to do. Where does that doubt come from and what's a good way to counter those thoughts when they come?

Jesus: First, you need to realize that you have an enemy, here on earth, and that your enemy is very real. You also need to realize that your enemy is not another man. Rather, your enemy is the great deceiver, thief, liar, and murderer. And you, right now, you are his primary target.

Your enemy has a primary tool to use against you, and that tool is to lie to you repeatedly. His goal is to get you to believe his lies. Because, if he can get you to believe his lies, he knows that you're not likely to become the man you were created to become. If he can get you to believe his lies, he can devour you, steal your future, and destroy your life.

Your enemy wants to take you out. He wants you to be weak and ineffective. He wants you to be doubting yourself and doubting others. He wants you to be afraid and timid. He wants to kill and destroy everything good and positive and loving in this world.

You must realize that you are the target - you are the principal target of his lies. He really does want to take you out.

With this realization, you must prepare for battle and fight back. You must fight for your future and your life. And then, when you do recognize that you have been targeted, and you're in the fight, never forget that I have your back. I am on your side - you are never fighting alone. I am here to give you a satisfying life.

Come to me when you feel under attack. Pray for wisdom to recognize the lies and read the scriptures when you do. Pray to the Father when you experience the assault. And always remember that you're never fighting alone, I am with you.

Scriptures:

1 Peter 5:8 "Stay alert! Watch out for your great enemy, the devil. He prowls around like a roaring lion, looking for someone to devour.

Matthew 4:10 "'Get out of here, Satan,' Jesus told him. 'For the Scriptures say You must worship the Lord your God, and serve only him.'"

John 10:10 "The thief's purpose is to steal and kill and destroy. My purpose is to give them a rich and satisfying life."

Ephesians 6:12 "For we are not fighting against flesh-and-blood enemies, but against evil rulers and authorities of the unseen world, against mighty powers in this dark world, and against evil spirits in the heavenly places."

Questions: Now that you realize you are Satan's primary target, are you ready to fight? Do you remember that Jesus has your back, and you're not fighting alone?

KNOW YOUR ENEMY

In your previous answer, you mentioned the enemy. I know this is something you've spoken about before. I also know this is something that many men have a hard time fully comprehending, at least I know that I do. Who exactly is this enemy, and why is he after me?

Jesus: Your enemy has gone by many names, over the years; names like the tempter, the devil, Beelzebub, Satan, and more. I have called him a liar, a murderer, the father of lies, the evil one, and the enemy. He is most definitely your enemy, and he has you in his sights to take you out.

The reason he is after you is because he hates who you're becoming, he hates that you're building this relationship with me, and he hates that you're on the path of doing what the Father created you to do. Your enemy needs to keep attacking you, to keep you small, to keep you from following your calling, and to keep you from leading others to me.

Just as any man in the military will tell you, you have to know your enemy in order to defeat your enemy. You have to know you're in the fight, in order to win the fight. Because, as simple as it sounds, the truth is that you're not going to win a fight that you don't even realize is happening.

And that's exactly what he wants. Your enemy wants you to doubt his very existence. Your enemy wants you to believe his lies. Your enemy wants you to think you don't have a chance to win. Your enemy wants you to give up. Your enemy wants you to feel like you're alone in the fight.

As I mentioned in the last answer and will repeat more, you are never fighting him alone, as I'm always by your side. When you're in the fight, you are to use the exact same weapons and defense I used when he was attacking me. The Word is your weapon, as it was mine. I countered every attack of the enemy with the Word

So when you feel the enemy's lies, change your focus to honoring and serving the Father. Learn to use the Scriptures in your daily life. Come to the Father in prayer. Do not fight alone – because you never are. Always remember that I am the warrior who fights by your side every minute of every day. I have your back.

Scriptures:

John 10:10 "The thief comes only to steal and kill and destroy. I came that they may have life and have it abundantly." (ESV)

1 Peter 5:8-9 "Be sober-minded; be watchful. Your adversary, the devil, prowls around like a roaring lion, seeking someone to devour. Resist him, firm in your faith, knowing that the same kinds of suffering are being experienced by your brotherhood throughout the world." (ESV)

Matthew 4:10 "Then Jesus said to him, 'Be gone, Satan! For it is written, 'You shall worship the Lord your God and him only shall you serve.'" (ESV)

Questions: In the Bible, Jesus very clearly indicated that Satan is real and specifically wanted to destroy men. Do you believe Jesus? What is one Scripture that you will memorize this week, to use when you feel you are under attack?

STAY IN THE FIGHT

There are lots of men who think that if they become a Christian, and if they just believe the right things, then suddenly their problems will go away. As I've learned myself, however, that is never the case. What do you say to a man who thinks following you is a crutch or the easy way to go?

Jesus: Following me is not easy, nor is it any form of crutch. Following me does not guarantee that there will be no problems, nor challenges, nor any difficulties in life. In fact, it's the exact opposite. Following me causes the enemy of this world to take notice of you and react, as he cannot stand it when good men choose to follow me.

For many men, it's only after I have saved them that they begin to experience the enemy's true attacks. Because once that man is saved, he becomes aware of his own nature and the bigger role he has to play. He becomes aware of the fact that there is a battle to fight. He becomes aware of who he can be and becomes aware of the work he needs to do to get there. So do not be deceived that simply because the man is blessed that he shall have no hardship or difficulty. One does not remove the other.

That is when it's critically important that he remains committed to the path he has chosen. When the battle comes, and it absolutely will, he is to remember that he's not fighting alone. When the challenges come, and they will, he is to remember to call on me. He is to remember to come to me.

During the challenges, engage in prayer. During the challenges, read the Scriptures. During the challenges, have another man walk by your side. During the challenges, stay in the fight.

The Father will bless every man who chooses to stay in the fight because of me. The Father smiles on every man who makes the hard choice to stand up for what is good and right and to stay in the fight, despite the challenges.

Those who follow me, those who strengthen their faith through the trials, will have their lives saved. It will not be easy, but those who do walk the walk will be eternally rewarded.

Scriptures:

Matthew 11:6 "And he added, 'God bless those who do not fall away because of me."

2 Timothy 3:12 "Yes, and everyone who wants to live a godly life in Christ Jesus will suffer persecution."

Luke 9:23-24 "Then he said to the crowd, 'If any of you wants to be my follower, you must give up your own way, take up your cross daily, and follow me. If you try to hang on to your life, you will lose it. But if you give up your life for my sake, you will save it."

Questions: When your battle comes, are you ready to stay in the fight? What does it mean to you that God will bless you when you stay in the fight?

STRONGHOLDS

Sometimes I'm trying to make a change, to get better in an area of my life, and I seem to keep spinning my wheels. I end up feeling like I'm getting nowhere, and that I'm just stuck in this one spot. I find myself repeatedly struggling with the same thing, and it's like I keep making the same mistakes over and over. These feelings can be overwhelming as if that one thing in my life will never change. How do I move forward when I feel stuck like that?

Jesus: This feeling of being stuck is often from incorrect thinking, not the reality of the situation. As we've talked about, your enemy uses lies as his primary attack against you. Those lies, when repeated over and over can start to form strongholds in your mind.

You start to think something is true, but it's a lie. The enemy of this world has taken hold of your thoughts and convinced you of this something that's simply not true. However, that lie has become so deeply ingrained in your thinking that you cannot even imagine your life without the lie.

The lie has become a stronghold in your mind. For men, these strongholds take many different forms. Three of the most common ones are pride, sex, and money, and sometimes a man is dealing with strongholds in all three of those at the same time.

Your enemy creates the lie and then reminds you about how you have failed in the past. He then whispers thoughts you know you shouldn't be thinking and uses language that is designed to make you reluctantly agree. Then you feel guilty for the thoughts, as if you are a failure, and the spiral deepens.

This is why I speak so passionately about guarding your heart. A hardened heart is very susceptible to strongholds. Always keep your heart focused on the truth, and fight against the lies. Since the stronghold is built upon lies, shining the light of truth directly on it is the way to fight back.

Use the scriptures in response to the lies. Pray in response to the lies. Shine a light of truth on the lies. Bring me in to fight alongside you, and you will destroy the strongholds.

Scriptures:

Proverbs 4:23 "Guard your heart above all else, for it determines the course of your life."

Philippians 4:8 "And now, dear brothers and sisters, one final thing. Fix your thoughts on what is true, and honorable, and right, and pure, and lovely, and admirable. Think about things that are excellent and worthy of praise."

2 Corinthians 10:4 "We use God's mighty weapons, not worldly weapons, to knock down strongholds of human reasoning and to destroy false arguments."

Ephesians 6:10-11 "A final word: Be strong in the Lord and in his mighty power. Put on all of God's armor so that you will be able to stand firm against all strategies of the devil."

Questions: Have you identified the strongholds that have taken root in your life? The next time you get stuck in the same area, what weapons will you use, and how will you use them, to break that stronghold?

REJECTION

One of the deepest fears of most men is rejection. It could be rejection from a girlfriend while dating, from a wife while married, from an employer while an employee, from a parent, from a friend, and so on. The fear of rejection keeps many men from taking action in the first place. Did you ever face rejection yourself? How should we deal with rejection?

Jesus: Yes, I faced rejection, even rejection from my own family. One time when I went home to teach and show people the way, those who saw and heard me refused to accept me. They were concerned with who my earthly father was, they were concerned with who my siblings were, and they rejected me. They were unable to see who I am and were only focused on who they thought I used to be.

People judged and rejected me because they knew I wasn't raised by wealthy parents. They judged and rejected me because they thought that I was only a carpenter. Instead of being able to hear my words, instead of being able to see me standing in front of them, they rejected me.

Your enemy uses the possibility of future rejection as a tool against you. Your enemy is planting the seeds of failure, telling you lies that you're never going to win or succeed, telling you lies that you shouldn't even try, and telling you lies that you will be rejected.

There will be people, throughout your life, who reject you, and you can't do anything about that. They will reject you because of where you went to school, or if you didn't go to school. They will reject you because of what you look like, or how you talk. They will reject you because of where you grew up. They will reject you because of your career choice. They will reject you because of someone else in your family. They will judge, mock, and reject you because of a whole host of reasons.

But I will never reject you. The Father will never reject you. Your life isn't about you being accepted by your fellow man; it's about your relationship with me and the Father. When you feel down due to rejection, remember that the Father is always with you and that He will strengthen you. Remember that God will provide you strength and will support you. Remember that I am always with you.

Scriptures:

Mark 6:4 "Then Jesus told them, 'A prophet is honored everywhere except in his own hometown and among his relatives and his own family.'"

Isaiah 41:10 "Don't be afraid, for I am with you. Don't be discouraged, for I am your God. I will strengthen you and help you. I will hold you up with my victorious right hand."

Questions: Did you know that Jesus was rejected, in his hometown, by people who knew him well? When you are feeling rejected, do you bring your concerns to Jesus and remember that he is with you?

EGO

We currently live in a very "I" and "me" society. From social media posts to politics, people love to take credit for what they are doing and have accomplished. It seems as if the ego of everyone, from individual men to global leaders, is inflating. The ego of a man is part of the man, so what should a man do with his ego?

Jesus: A man's ego is neither automatically good nor bad. However, for most men, their ego has a strong sense of pride and of self-importance. And when a man has an inflated sense of pride or an inflated sense of self-importance that's not a good thing.

Ego can lead to a false sense of who a man is; it can lead him to thinking that all he is, is due to himself. When a man's ego grows, it clouds his ability to see the truth, which is that everything comes from the Father. The man with the large ego is to remember that he did not create the very air that he breathes, nor did he create the very earth upon which his house sits.

The more that a man allows his ego to lead him, the more he will be unsatisfied. To appease his ego, he will be on the constant lookout for what he can do next. And, he will be anxious about what's coming that might disrupt what he has done. Which all means he will never experience peace and contentment.

For a man to experience peace and contentment, he must work to minimize his ego. He must work on his humility. He must work on softening his heart.

A humble man does not have room in his heart for inflated pride, inflated arrogance, or inflated self-importance. A humble man understands that what he has, who he is, and who he will become all come from the Father. A humble man honors the Father. A humble man can achieve great things, all while understanding that he did not get to where he is all by himself.

Scriptures:

John 5:30 "I can do nothing on my own. I will judge as God tells me. Therefore, my judgment is just, because I carry out the will of the one who sent me, not my own will."

Micah 6:8 "No, O people, the Lord has told you what is good, and this is what he requires of you: to do what is right, to love mercy, and to walk humbly with your God."

Romans 12:3 "Because of the privilege and authority God has given me, I give each of you this warning: Don't think you are better than you really are. Be honest in your evaluation of yourselves, measuring yourselves by the faith God has given us."

Questions: Has your ego ever gotten in the way of you doing what you know Jesus would want you to do? Are you able to drop your ego and acknowledge all you have is from God?

DAILY DISCIPLINE

Quite often when I read the Bible, or listen to a sermon, or have a deep conversation about faith, I find myself feeling like I don't really know much at all. I want to improve my understanding of you, of the Bible, and of God. And, I greatly want to grow in my faith. What's the best way for me to do this, how do I grow in these ways?

Jesus: What you're asking about is directly tied to your own spiritual discipline. Discipline seems like a loaded word these days, as most people often only associate it with punishment or correction. However, the discipline that matters for our conversation is the one that's all about training to produce a specific result.

Just like the best athletes, musicians, and craftsmen must have the discipline to train and improve, so must you in your spiritual journey. You have to work on building and practicing the behaviors that you need for your improvement, exactly as you would in your profession.

By working on your self-discipline, not only will you deepen your faith, but you will build up resistance and defense against the attacks of the world. Your daily discipline will become an integral part of how you deal with the lies of the enemy and stay focused on what the Father has called you to do.

You have two main areas where you can improve your daily discipline, prayer and Scripture. When you come to the Father in prayer, you are communicating your true self, your thoughts, your desires; you're asking for forgiveness, expressing your gratitude, and sharing your life. When the Father hears your honest and true prayers, he's proud of you. Ensure that you have time, every day, dedicated to prayer.

The other area is in knowing the Scriptures better. Study what is written. Examine how you can use what you learn in your own life. Share what you have learned with others. Memorize the word so that you can use it to counter the enemy's attacks, as I did myself.

When you add times of prayer and study of the Scriptures to your daily discipline, you will be on the path of producing what you're seeking.

Scriptures:

Joshua 1:8 "Study this Book of Instruction continually. Meditate on it day and night so you will be sure to obey everything written in it. Only then will you prosper and succeed in all you do."

1 Thessalonians 5:16-18 "Always be joyful. Never stop praying. Be thankful in all circumstances, for this is God's will for you who belong to Christ Jesus."

Hebrews 12:11 "No discipline is enjoyable while it is happening – it's painful! But afterward there will be a peaceful harvest of right living for those who are trained in this way."

Questions: How much time do you spend in prayer each day? How often do you read and study the Bible?

THE POWER OF ORDINARY MEN

I know I'm not alone in the struggle where I sometimes think that I'm not good enough. Even in having this conversation and writing this book, I feel the doubt creeping in since I'm just an ordinary man without any seminary degree. How should I deal with the issues of doubt that come along with feeling like I'm ordinary?

Jesus: My original twelve disciples were ordinary men, in the regard that they had no special training. They, in general, did not know the Scriptures all that well themselves. They had not been part of any religious leadership program. They didn't have theology degrees. They were average men who recognized who I was and who answered the call to follow.

That's what truly mattered; that they made the choice to follow me. They were men who had accepted me for who I am, as the Son of Man. They were men who understood the bigger picture, beyond themselves and their own stories.

And because my holy spirit lived within them, they were men who came to understand the incredible power they had been blessed with. These men, men without any prior awareness that their lives would head in this direction, found themselves out in the world performing miracles among the people. These ordinary men were doing powerful things they would never have imagined themselves doing.

Men who become my disciples today, who know me, who accept me, and who have faith in me, have also been blessed with incredible power. They know the power is not theirs, yet it flows through them.

My disciples, ordinary men and women, have the power to be truly free in this world, and to not be shackled by the world. My "ordinary" disciples have the power to achieve amazing results, to show their love to the world, to become a light for those in the darkness, and to lead people to me. Remember that you are just like the original disciples you read of in the Bible, and that you have that same power.

Scriptures:

Mark 6:12-13 "So the disciples went out, telling everyone they met to repent of their sins and turn to God. And they cast out many demons and healed many sick people, anointing them with olive oil."

Acts 4:13 "The members of the council were amazed when they saw the boldness of Peter and John, for they could see that they were ordinary men with no special training in the Scriptures. They also recognized them as men who had been with Jesus.

Galatians 4:9 "So now that you know God (or should I say, now that God knows you), why do you want to go back again and become slaves once more to the weak and useless spiritual principles of this world?"

Questions: Do you believe you have such power? Do you realize that you are no different from the original disciples, who were ordinary men? How are you using the power which flows through you?

RESPECT

If there was one thing that I know all men crave, it is respect. A man wants to be respected even when, and sometimes especially when, he makes mistakes. It can be a challenge to respect a man who is making mistakes or seems like he has not earned it, so how should we deal with such men?

Jesus: Yes, the word respect, by itself, can bring up powerful reactions in men. Men do crave respect, and they want to be shown respect in every situation. Men particularly crave respect from their wives.

As the Father created all people, all people are to be loved and respected. Men are to show respect for other men, even if, and sometimes especially when, those other men don't appear to deserve it. This is not done for the benefit of the other man; instead it's done for the benefit of the Father.

You are not to only show respect to those you agree with, or those who can provide you with something in return. Rather, you are to show respect to everyone, as they are all created by the Father. Respecting everyone shows the world that you are my follower and sets an example for all to see.

You desire respect yourself, even during the times when you make mistakes. Why would you not provide to other men the exact same thing that you desire for yourself? It's not about earning respect for yourself, it's about providing what your fellow men need, for them.

I respected my disciples, even when they weren't doing exactly what I might have wanted. My disciple Simon denied knowing me when I was arrested. Yet, when I first met him, I let him know that he would be known as Peter, the rock. I knew that by respecting the man, it would be a part of his process in growing into who the Father had created him to become.

An important key in you leading a man to becoming who he can be is to treat him with powerful respect, even when people may feel he has not yet earned it. Respect him, not because you have decided he deserved it, but instead because it's what the Father wants you to do. Respect him for the Father.

Scriptures:

1 Peter 2:17 "Respect everyone, and love the family of believers. Fear God and respect the king."

1 Thessalonians 5:12-13 "Dear brothers and sisters, honor those who are your leaders in the Lord's work. They work hard among you and give you spiritual guidance. Show them great respect and wholehearted love because of their work. And live peacefully with each other."

Matthew 16:18 "Now I say to you that you are Peter (which means 'rock'), and upon this rock I will build my church, and all the powers of hell will not conquer it."

Questions: How do you show respect to men who you feel have not yet earned it? How do you feel knowing that Jesus has respect for you, right now?

PROOF ENOUGH

There are men I talk with today who struggle to have faith because it cannot be scientifically proven. These are men who are "on the edge" so to speak. They are open-minded enough to listen but would say they cannot believe without proof. What kind of proof could you offer to such a man?

Jesus: People have doubted me since I first began teaching. Doubt is part of life. For people seeking specific proof, none will ever suffice; and for people who have faith, none will ever be required.

One time I headed back to my hometown to teach and perform miracles. There I was, in my hometown where everyone had seen me grow up, so they all knew who I used to be in the past. But, instead of being able to see and hear who I was, they mocked and scoffed at me for who they thought I should be.

Because they had known me in the past, they were unable to see who I was as I stood in front of them. Even my own earthly family and friends I had known for years made the choice not to believe. There could not have been any more proof than what was taking place right in front of them.

These were people, again including some of my own family, who were directly watching me, and directly listening to me, and yet they still made the choice not to believe. Clearly, seeing with their own eyes was not enough and hearing with their own ears was not enough for them to believe.

Yet, there were others, others who saw the exact same things and heard the exact same words, and they did believe. The difference was in their hearts, in their minds, and in their choice to believe.

By definition, faith requires belief in something that one cannot prove. All men do have faith in something when their views are pushed to the limits. So the choice then becomes what to believe in, the choice is where will they place their faith.

Men who choose to have faith in me and in the Father experience a life that is unavailable to those who choose the opposite, and there is no proof in existence that could change that.

Scriptures:

Matthew 13:16-17 "But blessed are your eyes, because they see; and your ears, because they hear. I tell you the truth, many prophets and righteous people longed to see what you see, but they didn't see it. And they longed to hear what you hear, but they didn't hear it."

Mark 6:3 "Then they scoffed, 'He's just a carpenter, the son of Mary and the brother of James, Joseph, Judas, and Simon. And his sisters live right here among us.' They were deeply offended and refused to believe him."

Questions: How do you feel about the fact that people watched and heard Jesus, in person, yet they still did not believe? Do you have anyone in your past who does not believe in the man you have become today?

LIFE ALONE

Some of the times in my life when I felt the most alone, were when I was walking through life all by myself. These were times when I felt that I had no one I could call or talk to, to figure out difficult situations with. I needed other men in my life, and I hadn't done the work to have them. Other times, men feel like they must prove themselves by being tough on their own and figuring out things on their own. Men are often very independent, so should a man go through life alone?

Jesus: There may be seasons when a man temporarily is alone, but it's unfortunate when men make a choice to go through life alone. The strongest man alive still needs others in his life. The smartest man alive still needs others in his life. Because man was not created to be alone. As we talked about earlier, when Adam walked the earth, he was in perfect union with God, and yet the Father told him that it was not good for him to be alone.

Even I had twelve men with me; I did not walk my walk on earth alone. I had my friends with me. In other words, while I had direct communication with my Father, it was still not enough for me - I needed other men by my side.

Life is not meant for you to try and go through it alone. Life is meant to be lived with others and to be shared with others. During the difficult and challenging times, being able to help one of your brothers is an incredibly powerful and positive thing. And the other side of the coin is equally true, knowing that you have brothers who will help you during your trials is an incredibly encouraging and comforting thing.

It's not a coincidence that your difficult times happen when you feel the most alone. The enemy has an easier time planting lies into your mind when you're alone. The enemy has an easier time attacking your values, your faith, and your relationship with me when you're alone. This is why the enemy lies to you about how it is ok for you to be alone. This is why the enemy lies to you about how you don't need other men in your life.

Men do need other men in their lives. You need other men who will lift you up when you're down, and other men you can lift up when they are down. It's very important for you to both have friends you can count on and be a friend that others can count on.

Scriptures:

John 15:13-14 "There is no greater love than to lay down one's life for one's friends. You are my friends if you do what I command."

John 11:2-3 "This is the Mary who later poured the expensive perfume on the Lord's feet and wiped them with her hair. Her brother, Lazarus, was sick. So, the two sisters sent a message to Jesus telling him, 'Lord, your dear friend is very sick.'"

Psalm 133:1 "How wonderful and pleasant it is when brothers live together in harmony!"

Questions: Have you ever thought about the fact that even Jesus had his friends by his side? How many men do you have who are walking the walk with you? If that number is less than you desire, what are you doing to change that?

FUNNY MAN

When I was growing up, I regularly felt like church was only a solemn place, no laughing, no humor, and always serious conversations. Honestly, it was boring and dull and didn't help me want to learn more or go deeper in my faith. I really enjoy laughing and having fun. Obviously, a church service isn't supposed to be a bunch of jokes or constant laughing, but it seems to me like some humor in church now and then is a good thing. Is it ok to laugh and have fun in church, or should that be a serious place all the time?

Jesus: I love laughter and great jokes. Humor is a wonderful gift to humanity. Sometimes it can be used to release pressure in a difficult situation, sometimes it can be used to lift people and bring them joy, and sometimes it can be used to walk people through stories.

I often used humor and irony in my parables with people. Unfortunately, there are times when the humor of my parables and the language of my time don't exactly translate to your language of today. And of course, when you are only reading you miss out on all the fun body language and expressions that go along with the text. You don't get my smirks, smiles, shrugs, and sideways glances when you're only reading the words on the pages.

So one has to be willing to see it, but I thought it was hysterical to talk in hyperbole about an actual plank in someone's eye, giving your children a snake or scorpion, a camel going through the eye of a needle, or even someone swallowing a camel! That's full of irony and is just plain funny to go along with teaching. Especially talking with the Pharisees; I liked using irony, wit, and sarcasm with those guys. I think those are great tools to make a point and make people smile at the same time.

It's lots of fun to laugh with my friends as well. One time I decided to give two of my disciples, brothers James and John, the nickname of the 'Sons of Thunder'. I thought that was pretty funny and the guys got a laugh out of that as well.

Laughing is an important part of life, something the world could use more of. And it's an important part of life whether you're inside a church building or outside one.

Scriptures:

Mark 3: 17 "James and John (the sons of Zebedee, but Jesus nicknamed them 'Sons of Thunder')"

Matthew 23:24 "Blind guides! You strain your water, so you won't accidentally swallow a gnat, but you swallow a camel!"

Luke 11:11 "You fathers – if your children ask for a fish, do you give them a snake instead? Or if they ask for an egg, do you give them a scorpion? Of course not!"

Questions: When reading the Bible, have you noticed the humor of Jesus? Are you able to think about him laughing and joking around with people? Do you need to bring more humor into your life? Is your church life only serious?

INTEGRITY

We live in a world where there seems to be an opportunity to do the wrong things, all the time. We have access to negative and damaging stuff online, stuff we could look at it when no one is around, and no one would know. We can see and find occasion to be dishonest almost everywhere we look. How do we maintain our integrity and do the right thing, when it often feels like the world is leading us in the opposite direction?

Jesus: A man who lives a life of high integrity is a man other people will want to be around, learn from, and simply enjoy the company of. However, it's not easy for most men to live their lives in a place of high integrity every day, although that is the goal. The reason it's tough is that the enemy of this world attempts to break men of their integrity at every chance he gets.

As a man of integrity, I want you to be faithful and true to what I have taught you. I want you to deepen your connection with the Father. I want you to shine your light, for the world to see. I want you to remember what I did when my integrity was tested.

After I was baptized, I needed time with the Father to prepare for what was coming next in my life. I went away by myself, into the wilderness, to fast and to pray. During this time Satan, the enemy, did come to me and repeatedly tried to get me to break my integrity. I prayed to the Father and used the word of God over and over during that time. So, I definitely understand what it's like to be tempted to drop your integrity and simply do the wrong things.

I would encourage you to do what I did. During those times, when you can feel the pull of this world on you to break your integrity, use your own weapons to fight back. Remember earlier when we talked about there being an enemy who wants to attack you and take you out? The pull to not be a man of integrity is part of that attack.

When that's happening, come to me, I'm always on your side. Pray to the Father; he is always listening. Read the scriptures, absorb and apply the wisdom in the book.

Scriptures:
Proverbs 10:9 "People with integrity walk safely, but those who follow crooked paths will be exposed."

Hebrews 4:14-15 "So then, since we have a great High Priest who has enter heaven, Jesus the Son of God, let us hold firmly to what we believe. This High Priest of ours understands our weaknesses, for he faced all of the same testings we do, yet he did not sin."

Isaiah 54:17 "But in that coming day, no weapon turned against you will succeed. You will silence every voice raised up to accuse you. These benefits are enjoyed by the servants of the Lord; their vindication will come from me. I, the Lord, have spoken!"

Psalm 15:5 "Those who lend money without charging interest, and who cannot be bribed to lie about the innocent. Such people will stand firm forever."

Questions: When you feel you are heading down the path of breaking your integrity, what do you normally do? Are you ready to use your weapons to fight back in this attack?

ANGER

When I was younger, I had a pretty bad temper. I would get upset at things from how people are driving on the roads to how customers were acting at the places I worked. Over the years I've calmed down, and that angry streak is gone, but this part of my past has made me wonder about you. Did you ever get angry, and what was that like for you?

Jesus: When I walked here on Earth, I experienced the full range of human emotion. I was not "above it all" as some people like to claim about me. And that means that yes, there were definitely times when I got angry.

What people sometimes get confused about is to think that anger, itself, is bad. That's not the case. Nowhere is a man instructed never to be angry. He will not read that in the ten commandments. He will not hear that from me.

The key is to be aware of what it is that you get angry about, and never to let your anger control you. If you let your anger control you, you're in a dangerous place, a place that the enemy will use. Uncontrolled anger gives your enemy a way into your heart.

You'll notice that my anger was towards what people did. When I saw what was happening in the temple, I was most definitely angry at those actions. I took my time, made myself a weapon, and then went into the Temple to clear everyone out and put a stop to what they were doing.

Another time, I noticed a man with a deformed hand. The religious leaders of the time had forbidden any work to be done on the Sabbath. I asked them if evil was still allowed on that day, and asked if, instead, that day was for saving a life?

When they didn't respond, I took the man's hand and healed him. I was angry and saddened by what had happened to their hearts. Their eyes and their hearts were unable to see and know the bigger picture, which did make me angry.

Do not allow yourselves to be angry with the person. If you're going to be angry, be angry with their sins, their actions, or with what they are doing. But, not the person, for everyone is a child of the Father.

Scriptures:

Mark 3:5 "He looked around at them angrily and was deeply saddened by their hard hearts. Then he said to the man, 'Hold out your hand.' So the man held out his hand, and it was restored!"

John 2:15 "Jesus made a whip from some ropes and chased them all out of the Temple. He drove out the sheep and cattle, scattered the money changers' coins over the floor, and turned over their tables."

Ephesians 4:26-27 "And 'Don't sin by letting anger control you.' Don't let the sun go down while you are still angry, for anger gives a foothold to the devil."

Questions: If Jesus were to look inside your heart, would he see anything that would make him angry? Has your anger ever taken control over your words or actions? If so, how could you gain that control?

RESTING

I have so many things I want to get done, and my list of projects seems to keep growing every day. I find it difficult, at times, just to get away and rest. In our 24/7 world, it seems like resting becomes more and more elusive. Other guys I talk to tell me about how they also feel guilty when they take any time at all for themselves. How do I know when I need to take a break and get some rest?

Jesus: Even the Father, after his work of creation, took a day to rest, so you can start by remembering that. He looked at all that he had done, and took a day to rest, declaring that day holy. When Moses delivered the ten commandments, included was to keep the Sabbath day as a holy day.

Resting is important for all men. You need physical rest, and you need spiritual rest. You need time for your body to recover and recharge. You need time for your spirit to recover and recharge. Without rest, a man can quickly become burnt-out, stressed, and overwhelmed with the life he is living. My own disciples went through this as well.

They had just come back to me from doing great work, throughout the land. They had been teaching and healing, and they were exhausted. I could see it in their eyes and suggested we all take the boat out and get away for a while. Clearly, they needed a break, they needed some rest, and a get-away trip with the guys seemed exactly like the way to go.

When you are starting to feel the burden and feel like you're unable to rest, that's when you need to come to me. I'm waiting for you to share your weariness with me so that I can take that burden off your shoulders and carry it for you.

Taking some time, even in the middle of a busy day, to study the word and come to the Father in prayer is an excellent way to make it through those long days. Learn from the scriptures. Learn from me. Allow me to carry that burden for you, so that you may find some rest in your soul.

Scriptures:

Mark 6:30-32 "The apostles returned to Jesus from their ministry tour and told him all they had done and taught. Then Jesus said, 'Let's go off by ourselves to a quiet place and rest awhile.' He said this because there were so many people coming and going that Jesus and his apostles didn't even have time to eat. So they left by boat for a quiet place, where they could be alone."

Genesis 2:2-3 "On the seventh day God had finished his work of creation so he rested from all his work. And God blessed the seventh day and declared it holy, because it was the day when he rested from all his work of creation."

Matthew 11:28-29 "Then Jesus said, 'Come to me, all of you who are weary and carry heavy burdens, and I will give you rest. Take my yoke upon you. Let me teach you, because I am humble and gentle at heart, and you will find rest for your souls.'"

Questions: How often do you take time away to rest? Do you find yourself feeling guilty when you take time for yourself to rest? What burden are you carrying, right now, that you can share with Jesus so that you will find rest for your soul?

EVEN ME?

In this gigantic universe, sometimes I feel like it isn't realistic for you to even know me, let alone think about me and what I'm going through. Compared to the big pain and suffering we see, from the devastation of a hurricane, a famine, or a disease that impacts millions, sometimes it seems like my problems are too small to matter. Do you really know and care for every human here on Earth?

Jesus: I understand how overwhelming this can feel. The logical side of our brains would say that such a thing is impossible; yet, here we are talking with one another. Yes, I know and care for every man, woman, and child.

There was a time when I was teaching a whole crowd, and some men brought me their friend. Which, by the way, was pretty awesome; I love it when men lead their friends to me. Anyway, this friend was deaf and had speech difficulty. So even though the crowd was there, I stepped away with just this man, to be alone with him and to heal him. I did this because every single person matters to me. Every single person is important to me. Every single person can have time with me. Every single person is loved by me. Every single person is known by the Father.

You are important to me. You can have time with me. You are loved by me. You are known by the Father.

Imagine for a moment that you were blessed with 100 children. With that many kids, you would undoubtedly have lots of sleepless nights, that's for sure. But, in the midst of the chaos of such a household, you would also deeply love each of those children. Now imagine that one day you were playing in the yard with your kids and you realized that one was missing, what would you do?

You would go after your one missing child. You would seek high and low until your child was returned safely back home. It's no different with the Father. Every single one of his children is important to him, and he will rejoice for every single one that is home safe with him.

Scriptures:

Mark 7:32-33 "A deaf man with a speech impediment was brought to him, and the people begged Jesus to lay his hands on the man to heal him. Jesus led him away from the crowd so they could be alone..."

Ephesians 1:4 "Even before he made the world, God loved us and chose us in Christ to be holy and without fault in his eyes."

Matthew 18:14 "In the same way, it is not my heavenly Father's will that even one of these little ones should perish."

Jeremiah 1:5 "I knew you before I formed you in your mother's womb. Before you were born I set you apart and appointed you as my prophet to the nations."

Questions: Do you believe that you matter to Jesus? Do you remember that he has time for you, every time you need him to? Are you leading your friends to Jesus?

SHARE YOUR POWER

Too often on the news, we hear of a leader who seemed to be fully in control of his company or career, and who crashed back to Earth. He was the man in charge, no questions asked. He was the man who squashed any opposition and made sure no one could ever threaten his position. What could these men have done differently, to avoid the hard crash-landing they went through?

Jesus: Two parts to this one. First, when men become overly focused on power, it can very easily and quickly become an idol to them. The idol of power is very alluring to many men. The enemy likes using idols to perpetuate lies, keep men off track, and keep them from focusing on the Father and me.

This is one reason that men have to be very careful when it comes to power. These men end up consumed by obtaining more and more power, frequently using that power to control other people. Their hearts then become hardened to anything that does not increase their own personal power.

Inevitably this does lead to the crash, because the idol of power, like all false idols, will never sustain life, only take it away. Men who are seeking to avoid that crash need to replace the idol with the Father.

The second part is that this kind of man is unable to share his power. He fears giving away his power, fears that he may lose control, and fears that he can no longer force people to do his bidding. Those fears are lies, but such a man will believe the lies and be fearful of sharing his power.

Just as I gave my power to my disciples, and as I continue to share my power to all who follow me, any man who leads others need to give and share his power with those he leads. Men need to empower the people around them, lifting those other people up to greater heights.

Men who are seeking to avoid the crash need to make sure they don't turn power into an idol, and they need to share their power. Whether this happens naturally, or with conscious effort, sharing their power is a trait that all great leaders have in common.

Scriptures:

Luke 9:1 "One day Jesus called together his twelve disciples and gave them power and authority to cast out all demons and to heal all diseases."

Acts 1:8 "But you will receive power when the Holy Spirit comes upon you. And you will be my witnesses, telling people about me everywhere – in Jerusalem, throughout Judea, in Samaria, and to the ends of the earth."

1 John 5:21 "Dear children, keep away from anything that might take God's place in your hearts."

Questions: Have you ever felt the pull of the idol of power? Are you able to share the spotlight? How does it impact you when others around you have success, even if that success seems to be greater than your own? What have you done with the power that Jesus has shared with you?

LIVE FOR TODAY

When I start to get too focused on what I want to have happen later in life, I notice that I tend to get anxious about the future. When I spend too much time thinking about what might happen next year, I notice that I tend to get apprehensive about what that future will be like. What is a good way to balance looking forward while staying grounded in today at the same time?

Jesus: There's nothing wrong with planning for the future. It would be unwise to have no plan whatsoever, even more so when you have a family that is relying on you to lead them and provide for them. However, when a man becomes overly consumed by creating plans for the future or becomes overly concerned about what is going to happen next week, next year, or next decade, he's losing sight of what's in front of his eyes today.

No man is guaranteed to even see the sunset tonight, let alone future years in his life. No man is guaranteed even to know what tomorrow will hold for him, no matter how much he plans or how detailed he makes his plans.

The Father alone knows what tomorrow will bring. Only the Father knows how many more sunsets a man has left to experience in his life. Only the Father knows what your future looks like.

One way to keep all of this in balance is to consider which is greater in your mind: appreciating the day you've been given today, or planning for the next decade? When you spend more time being concerned about the future than you do in gratitude for today, you are shifting out of balance. Recognize when that happens and correct your course.

Change your focus so that you spend more time living today than you do planning for the future. Today is your day to show kindness and grace to others. Today is your day to be loving and to help those in need. Today is your day to defend those who cannot defend themselves. That is today.

Scriptures:

James 4:13-15 "Look here, you who say, 'Today or tomorrow we are going to a certain town and will stay there a year. We will do business there and make a profit.' How do you know what your life will be like tomorrow? Your life is like the morning fog - it's here a little while, then it's gone. What you ought to say is, 'If the Lord wants us to, we will live and do this or that.'"

Psalm 103:15-16 "Our days on earth are like grass; like wildflowers, we bloom and die. The wind blows, and we are gone – as though we had never been here."

Matthew 6:34 "So don't worry about tomorrow, for tomorrow will bring its own worries. Today's trouble is enough for today."

Ecclesiastes 5:15 "We all come to the end of our lives as naked and empty-handed as on the day we were born. We can't take our riches with us."

Questions: What is stopping you from appreciating every day as the gift that it is? If you were able to live with gratitude for each day, how would that impact your outlook on life?

UNQUALIFIED TO DREAM

When I'm talking with men, about something they want to pursue or some business they want to create, frequently it comes up that they feel unqualified to follow that dream. These are men who believe that because they don't have the right degree, background, or experience they are not qualified and often end up never following their dreams. How can a man overcome the feeling that he is simply unqualified to pursue his dream?

Jesus: Earlier I mentioned how the enemy of this world wants to keep men down; because the enemy is thrilled when men do not follow their dreams or when they choose to remain small. The idea that a man isn't qualified to become the man he was created to become is quite simply a lie.

No man is truly qualified, and every professional was once an amateur. Sometimes that man finds himself in a situation he never even could have imagined. He may find himself involved in a story that never crossed his mind.

Take my own disciples, for example. These men were from all parts of our society, from fishermen, to craftsmen, and even a tax collector. According to the religious leaders of the time, none of these men had any qualifications to become who they became. None of them were devoted students of the scriptures. None of them were noted for their ability to deliver a sermon or to teach crowds.

Yet, they made the choice to drop what they were doing and to follow me. And, when they did that, their entire lives were changed. They found themselves in a story they never predicted.

The same is true for you. You were created for a reason; you have a purpose. The enemy is trying to keep you away from your purpose, and the unqualified lie is one of his tricks. Do not fall for that trick, do not believe that lie. Stay on path to following the purpose you were given.

Know that I will give you the strength, and the Father will give you the qualifications. Because, the Father does not call the qualified, he qualifies the called.

Scriptures:

Acts 4:13 "The members of the council were amazed when they saw the boldness of Peter and John, for they could see that they were ordinary men with no special training in the Scriptures. They also recognized them as men who had been with Jesus."

Philippians 4:13 "For I can do everything through Christ, who gives me strength."

1 Corinthians 1:26-27 "Remember, dear brothers and sisters, that few of you were wise in the world's eyes or powerful or wealthy, when God called you. Instead, God chose things the world considers foolish in order to shame those who think they are wise. And he chose things that are powerless to shame those who are powerful."

Questions: Do you ever feel like you are unqualified to pursue your dreams, or to fulfill your calling? What do you think about the fact that Jesus chose unqualified men to be among his closest friends?

KNOWING MY PURPOSE

I often spend time after a week of working feeling like it was a wasted week. Like I just spent all my time working on someone else's company to create someone else's product to build someone else's dream. It barely feels like a purposeful or useful week for me. Yes, it provides for my family, but ends up feeling so shallow and empty most days. You just mentioned purpose in a previous answer, but how do I know what my life's purpose is?

Jesus: This is a question that men have been asking for centuries. Solomon, who many refer to as the wisest man who ever lived on Earth, pursued this question for a long time. After years of study, he learned that living for the things that this world holds dear, such as money or power, ultimately leads a man to an empty life. He concluded that the true purpose of a man is to live a life that honors and obeys the Father.

When men equate their means of providing an income with their purpose, this confusion becomes greater. Neither the career nor the level of income any man produces will ever define him in my eyes or in the eyes of the Father.

Another wise man, King David, learned that this world was not the limit to where he would find contentment. He knew that there was more than simply what would take place here, and he came to realize that his true satisfaction and joy would come when he opened his eyes to see, and have fellowship with, the Father.

Solomon and King David were clearly different, because every man has unique gifts, skills, talents, and abilities; and will therefore have a unique direction in his life. However, every man also shares commonalities; which is how those two wise men, whose paths never crossed, came to the same fundamental conclusion about purpose.

What this means is that knowing your purpose is directly connected to deepening your faith. As your faith grows, your purpose becomes clearer. When you are feeling that your purpose is unclear, bring that concern to the Father, and allow him to speak to you.

Scriptures:

Ecclesiastes 12:13-14 "That's the whole story. Here now is my final conclusion: Fear God and obey his commands, for this is everyone's duty. God will judge us for everything we do, including every secret thing, whether good or bad."

Psalm 17:15 "Because I am righteous, I will see you. When I awake, I will see you face to face and be satisfied."

Questions: Are you able to separate your career from your purpose, as a man? How will you deepen your faith, as a means to clarify your purpose?

SAY WHAT?

Right now, it's popular for men to speak what's on their minds, in all situations. It's the current trend for men to use whatever language they want, in any and all situations. This is done under the umbrella term of being authentic. How can a man remain true and authentic, while also controlling his language?

Jesus: Everyone is certain to make mistakes in this life, and everyone is certain to say things they will later regret saying. Controlling the tongue is one of the most difficult challenges for all people. If a man came up with a way to perfectly control what he says, every time he speaks, that man would be able to control everything about him. Of course, the reality is that's an impossible task for people.

The challenge is to use your words in a positive manner, to speak life into others, instead of pulling them down. Because, nothing can do more damage or more life-giving than what you say. With just a few words you could inspire people to greatness or could extinguish their dreams. Your words have incredible power.

Think of how the captain of a giant ship can turns the boat, just by using the small rudder. Think of how a single spark can set an entire forest on fire. Your tongue is like that; you can change the direction of your life, or other people's lives, with the words you choose to use.

Speaking negative, hurtful, or evil language, under the pretense of being authentic isn't an acceptable use of your power of words, and it shows what truly lies within your heart. On the other hand, if your heart is focused on love and being a positive influence, then that is what is authentic to you.

So learn to authentically listen more, and speak less. Learn to authentically think what it is you wish to say, before you say it. Learn to authentically use the power of your words to encourage and lift other people up on their walks through life.

Scriptures:

Proverbs 17: 27-28 "A truly wise person uses few words; a person with understanding is even-tempered. Even fools are thought wise when they keep silent; with their mouths shut, they seem intelligent."

Ephesians 4:29 "Don't use foul or abusive language. Let everything you say be good and helpful, so that your words will be an encouragement to those who hear them."

Matthew 12:36-37 "And I tell you this, you must give an account on judgment day for every idle word you speak. The words you say will either acquit you or condemn you."

James 4:11 "Don't speak evil against each other, dear brothers and sisters. If you criticize and judge each other, then you are criticizing and judging God's law. But your job is to obey the law, not to judge whether it applies to you."

Questions: Have you ever caught yourself saying something "authentic", only to regret it later? How could you change your speech patterns to use your words in a positive and encouraging manner?

LIMITLESS

There are times when I'm trying to do something, and I feel like it isn't appropriate for me to ask for your help. Sometimes it feels too small to bring you into the mix, and other times I'm too embarrassed by my lack of knowledge or by what I'm dealing with. How do I know when it's the right time to involve you in what I'm going through?

Jesus: It's always the right time to involve me. There is never a time when you shouldn't bring me into the situation. Period.

Men make a mistake when they feel like they shouldn't involve me. Men make a mistake when they try to put me in a box, as if there are situations where I can be involved, and then other situations where I can't be involved. Or as if there are situations I can help with, and others where I cannot. That's never true. Involve me in every situation, as there are none that are new to me, and are none that I cannot help with.

With your faith in me, anything is possible, there are no limits. I once walked on water to meet my disciples in their boat. One of my guys, Peter, was questioning what I was doing, so I told him to walk out on the water and join me. He was walking towards me, doing something that should be impossible, because he was focused on his faith. But then, he took his eyes off me, and noticed the wind and the waves, and he began to sink. He had put a limit on what was possible, and he had put a limit on his faith.

When you put limits on what I can achieve, or when put parts of your life off-limits to me, you're not living the full life you were created to live. Choose to bring me into all situations of your life and allow the power of the Father to flow through you. It doesn't matter if you think the issue is too big or too small, I'm here for you in the same way today as I was yesterday as I will be tomorrow. I'm ready for you, all you need to do is ask.

Scriptures:

Matthew 14:29-31 "Yes, come,' Jesus said. So Peter went over the side of the boat and walked on the water toward Jesus. But when he saw the strong wind and the waves, he was terrified and began to sink. 'Save me, Lord!' he shouted. Jesus immediately reached out and grabbed him. 'You have so little faith,' Jesus said. 'Why did you doubt me?'"

Hebrews 13:8 "Jesus Christ is the same yesterday, today, and forever."

Matthew 9:28-29 "They went right into the house where he was staying, and Jesus asked them, 'Do you believe I can make you see?' 'Yes, Lord,' they told him, 'we do.' Then he touched their eyes and said, 'Because of your faith, it will happen.'"

Luke 4:18-19 "The Spirit of the Lord is upon me, for he has anointed me to bring Good News to the poor. He has sent me to proclaim that captives will be released, that the blind will see, that the oppressed will be set free, and that the time of the Lord's favor has come."

Questions: What limits have you placed on Jesus? What areas of your life have you placed off-limits to Jesus?

WHO YOU ARE

It's so easy to get overwhelmed in this world, to start to feel small and insignificant. It's so easy to become consumed by the daily list of things that have to get done, that it becomes common for men to lose focus on their own identity. We can start to feel like our only purpose is to earn a paycheck for our families, and not much else. How can a man stay clear on who he really is?

Jesus: First and foremost, keep the Father's opinion of you in the highest regard, for his opinion is above all others. He knows you, and he loves you. You're a man who was fearfully and wonderfully made by him, exactly as you are. His view of you will not change if you drove a different car. His view of you will not change if you lived in a different house. He loves you, as you are.

The world decides who people are by their level of worldly success, the Father does not. You are not your car. You are not your career. You are not your house. You are not the balance of your bank account. None of those define who you are to the Father.

The enemy lies to you about who you are. The liar tries to define you by your mistakes, your sins, your failings. The liar tries to make you think that you will be known by all you have done in the past. But, that is not how you are defined by the Father.

Men tend to make this issue much more complicated than it needs to be. There are personality tests, profiles to examine, family histories to unpack, all trying to figure out who people are. In that list, notice that the scriptures are missing. The answer to who you are has already been written for you.

When you start to lose focus on who you are, go to the Father in prayer. Spend time away from distractions and be with him. If you are able to, get out in nature to connect with me. If you are unable, remove all the distractions around you and dedicate time alone with the Father and in reading the scriptures. Open your eyes and your mind to what you're reading.

As a man who follows me, you have been made new. You are a son of God. You are a man. You are a warrior.

That is who you are.

Scriptures:

1 Corinthians 1:30 "God has united you with Christ Jesus. For our benefit God made him to be wisdom itself. Christ made us right with God; he made us pure and holy, and he freed us from sin."

Psalm 139:14 "Thank you for making me so wonderfully complex! Your workmanship is marvelous – how well I know it."

2 Corinthians 5:17 "This means that anyone who belongs to Christ has become a new person. The old life is gone; a new life has begun!"

Questions: Who do you think that Jesus says you are? Have you heard the enemy's lies about who you are? When you start to feel like you are losing perspective about who you are, do you bring that concern to the Father?

A STRONG MAN

When I think of a man being strong, I think of a man who works out frequently, a man with lots of muscles, a man who is physically strong. Recently I've heard and read more about men being spiritually strong. What does that mean, and for an average guy like me, what does that look like in my life?

Jesus: It's important for men to be physically strong, if they're able. Physical strength is part of protecting your family, your friends, and others in need. But physical strength isn't the limit of how you should be strong, nor is it even the most important type of strength for you to possess.

It doesn't matter how physically strong you are, if you're spiritually weak. It doesn't matter if you can lift the heaviest weights, if you cannot lift your family in faith-filled prayer. Yes, you need to continue to train your physical strength, and you also need to train your spiritual strength. An example of a man who was both physically strong and spiritually strong was David.

When David was a young boy, he never had the physical strength to defeat Goliath. Yet he had spiritual strength and was victorious against all logic and against all odds. The same boy as a man, when he was not using his spiritual strength, was physically strong and he committed adultery and conspired to have a man killed. The same person lived both sides of the story of strength.

Your spiritual strength is what you use during the trials of life. Your spiritual strength is where you have true power, granted to you by the Father. Your spiritual strength is what you use to defend yourself, your family, and others when they are attacked by the enemy.

Because it doesn't matter how physically strong you are, without spiritual strength you will fall when tempted. Your spiritual strength is found in growing your faith, and in your relationship with me. Through me, there is nothing you can't do. When you let go of your ego enough to walk through life with me, you will experience spiritual strength.

Scriptures:

Isaiah 40:29-31 "He gives power to the weak and strength to the powerless. Even youths will become weak and tired, and young men will fall in exhaustion."

Philippians 4:13 "For I can do everything through Christ, who gives me strength."

2 Timothy 2:1 "Timothy, my dear son, be strong through the grace that God gives you in Christ Jesus."

Psalm 138:3 "As soon as I pray, you answer me; you encourage me by giving me strength."

Psalm 18:1-2 "I love you, Lord; you are my strength. The Lord is my rock, my fortress, and my savior; my God is my rock, in whom I find protection. He is my shield, the power that saves me, and my place of safety."

Ephesians 6:10 "A final word: Be strong in the Lord and in his mighty power."

Questions: How are you working out to improve your spiritual strength? Have you been willing to let go of your ego and submit to Jesus as your savior?

HOLD ME TO IT

Earlier we talked about the fact that men should not go through life without other men by their sides. For me, I've found that having a friend who can hold me accountable is a big help. Accountability is different than friendship or companionship, so what is the importance of accountability?

Jesus: Having another man by your side, a man who will hold you to account, is extremely important. And this is something that's sorely lacking in most of your culture. Notice how often, throughout history, men have been tempted and made bad decisions when they were alone or without an accountability partner by their side.

I mentioned how even King David was tempted with lust, committed adultery, and had a man's death arranged. During that time, he was without a brother to hold him back, to remind him of the right thing to do, or to stop him from falling down.

When you choose to fight alone, you're decreasing your odds -and your enemy likes that. Your enemy will tell you that it's too hard to find a good man to walk the walk with. Your enemy will tell you that you're too broken, or that you've done such horrible things, that no good man would ever want to walk the walk by your side. Those are all lies.

You're not too broken for another man to stand with you. You're not so far gone that no one will want to support you. Those are all lies.

The fact is that by having someone who will have your back, you're increasing your odds of living the life the Father created for you. I love it when you are willing to walk through life with another man by your side. I love it when you are willing to be that man for one of your brothers.

And another fact is that you will be held to account for what you do in this life. You will be held to account for what you believe in this life. You will be held accountable to your fellow man, to me, and to the Father. So live together in such a way that you are helping one another and living the life that you were called to live.

Scriptures:

Ecclesiastes 4:9-10 "Two people are better off than one, for they can help each other succeed. If one person falls, the other can reach out and help. But someone who falls alone is in real trouble."

Galatians 6:1-2 "Dear brothers and sisters, if another believer is overcome by some sin, you who are godly should gently and humbly help that person back onto the right path. And be careful not to fall into the same temptation yourself."

Romans 14:12-13 "Yes, each of us will give a personal account to God. So let's stop condemning each other. Decide instead to live in such a way that you will not cause another believer to stumble and fall."

Questions: Who are the men who hold you accountable? Who are the men who count on you to hold them to account? What areas of your life have you kept off-limits from them?

I FEEL IT'S RIGHT

A bit of a trend in our society right now is to think that just because we strongly feel something, it must be accepted as right. It's a difficult one to talk about, because the conversation is placed in the context of love, compassion, understanding, and caring, so anyone who does not automatically agree is called a hater or intolerant. What part of our feelings should determine what we do, or how we live our lives?

Jesus: The world enjoys living with feelings as the basis of an action, a choice, or a lifestyle as feelings are always changing and can therefore be shaped, manipulated, or molded to fit any viewpoint of the moment. Spiritual truth however, does not change, it's not something that's reshaped over and over to fit any current issue. While people may choose to interpret that truth differently at different times, the truth is the truth. The truth is that there are many things the world says yes to, that I say no to.

There's a constant fight taking place between my truth and the feelings of the world. When the world wants you to go in one direction, and when you notice deep in your soul that you should be going the other direction, take that other path. I love it when people stand up and do what's right, even when it's not popular, and even when those people know they will not be viewed well because of it.

I certainly understand that it's not easy to take a stand and go in an opposite direction from the ways of the world. This is why those who know me and follow me have experienced the full range of negativity from being mocked and called names like hater all the way to being murdered as a martyr.

When one makes the choice to act based on feelings, they're not living the life that they were created to live. Every day people have choices to make, and when those choices are based on feelings, frequently they're not going to be based on the truth that I have taught. And remember, I see and rejoice for every person who takes a stand, for me and the Father, for the truth.

Scriptures:

Matthew 5:11-12 "God blesses you when people mock you and persecute you and lie about you and say all sorts of evil things against you because you are my followers. Be happy about it! Be very glad! For a great reward awaits you in heaven. And remember, the ancient prophets were persecuted in the same way."

Galatians 5: 16-17 "So I say, let the Holy Spirit guide your lives. Then you won't be doing what your sinful nature craves. The sinful nature wants to do evil, which is just the opposite of what the Spirit wants. And the Spirit gives us desires that are the opposite of what the sinful nature desires. These two forces are constantly fighting each other, so you are not free to carry out your good intentions."

1 John 4:5-6 "Those people belong to this world, so they speak from the world's viewpoint, and the world listens to them. But we belong to God, and those who know God listen to us. If they do not belong to God, they do not listen to us. That is how we know if someone has the Spirit of truth or the spirit of deception."

Questions: Where have you allowed your feelings to impact your actions? When was the last time you took a stand for something you know is truth and which runs counter to the ways of the world?

FREEDOM

In most Western societies we take our freedom for granted while in much of the rest of the world most have never experienced freedom. That makes the concept of freedom challenging, when much of the world takes something for granted that much of the rest of the world hasn't experienced. Since billions do not know the freedom of the West, how can those people know freedom in their lifetimes?

Jesus: It's important to not confuse or conflate governmental freedom with spiritual freedom and the freedom that I offer. Many of the rulers of this world, all throughout human history, have sought to enslave people to do their bidding. And many thought that when I first walked on Earth that had I come to do battle with those rulers, in order to make people free from their governments.

However, the victory and freedom that I offer is entirely different. The freedom I offer is everlasting life and release from the bondage of sin. Even in a society which has governmental freedom, many men find themselves completely enslaved to their sins, corruption, and the ways of the world.

A man can live under a government which guarantees freedom for its citizens, and he can be fully enslaved to his sin. While at the exact same time, another man can live as a slave under the tyrannical rule of a leader, and he can be freed through me.

In other words, the government or ruler that one lives under does not determine the freedom of the man, rather his relationship with me does. I came to set people free, free from their sins and free into the glory of the Father's Kingdom.

To experience the freedom that I offer, one is to learn and follow the Father's word, ask for forgiveness of his sins, and believe in me as the Savior. That can be done, by any man, at any time. Even a man in prison can come to me and experience victory and freedom.

Scriptures:

John 3:16 "For this is how God loved the world: He gave his one and only Son, so that everyone who believes in him will not perish but have eternal life."

John 8:36 "So if the Son sets you free, you are truly free."

2 Corinthians 3:17 "For the Lord is the Spirit, and wherever the Spirit of the Lord is, there is freedom."

Psalm 119:45 "I will walk in freedom, for I have devoted myself to your commandments."

Romans 8:1-2 "So now there is no condemnation for those who belong to Christ Jesus. And because you belong to him, the power of the life-giving Spirit has freed you from the power of sin that leads to death."

2 Peter 2:19 "They promise freedom, but they themselves are slaves of sin and corruption. For you are a slave to whatever controls you."

Questions: Do you walk through life as the free man that you are? What does the freedom that Jesus offers you mean to you, in your everyday life?

EXHAUSTED

Years ago, when I was a young entrepreneur, I would be proud of how much I worked. I even had a cot in my office, telling myself I couldn't afford to waste time driving back and forth between home and work. In hindsight now, I see how much of a mistake that was, and the inevitable burnout happened. I know that risk of exhaustion is common in many men, so what should a man do to avoid burning out?

Jesus: In the culture of today the demands of the world continue to increase the pressure that men feel. You have pressure at home, pressure at work, pressure with friends, pressure at church, even pressure while relaxing, there's pressure everywhere! It's no surprise that so many men end up exhausted.

However, it's very important to step back and see where all that pressure is coming from. Those pressures come from the world, not from me or the Father. Your enemy is whispering lies into your mind that if you don't keep going full speed on all those things, all the time, that somehow, you're a failure. Your enemy tells you that if you don't provide the next great vacation for your family, that you're a failure. Your enemy, like always, is lying to you.

When you start to feel burned out, it's often because you have taken the weight of the world onto your shoulders and believed the lie that it's all up to you. You start to feel like only you can do it, you're the only one able to accomplish all the great things you're setting out to do. These are lies from the enemy.

The way to avoid burnout is to start by accepting the truth that the pressure you feel comes from your enemy. Learn to recognize those lies. Once you do that, then your eyes can see, and your ears can hear, what I have to show and teach you. Like we talked about earlier, you need rest. You need to stop thinking that it's all about you and all up to you.

Come to me, be willing to let me into your life so that I can walk with you, especially during your trials. Spend time, every day, in prayer. Focus on what the Father has called you to do, instead of what the world has. Rest your soul and experience the peace, joy, and contentment that I have come to offer.

Scriptures:

Mark 1:35 "Before daybreak the next morning, Jesus got up and went out to an isolated place to pray."

Mark 6:31-32 "Then Jesus said, 'Let's go off by ourselves to a quiet place and rest awhile.' He said this because there were so many people coming and going that Jesus and his apostles didn't even have time to eat."

Galatians 6:9 "So let's not get tired of doing what is good. At just the right time we reap a harvest of blessing if we don't give up."

Matthew 11:28 "Then Jesus said, 'Come to me, all of you who are weary and carry heavy burdens, and I will give you rest.'"

Questions: What is it you're seeking to accomplish or prove by being so busy? If Jesus needed to take time to get away, to rest, to pray, and to connect with the Father, how important is it that you do the same? How did Jesus model rest in a way that you can follow?

INSECURITY

Most of the time, I'm my own worst critic. Despite my best efforts and intentions, people post negative things about me and my work online, but that's nothing compared to the negative things I hear in my own head. When I'm nearing a goal, those negative things often become much louder, and I become much less sure of myself or what I am working towards. What should I do during those times when I can feel this insecurity pulling me down?

Jesus: First, remember that those negative things you hear are not coming from you. Those ideas of being unsure and insecure are not coming from you. They are coming from the enemy, who lies to you and who uses your own thoughts and words against you.

When you start to put your trust, and your faith, into the things of this world, that's when the lies from the enemy will lead towards insecurity. When you start to trust someone or something here on Earth, you have taken your eyes off the Father and away from my teaching, and that's when the lies of insecurity will start to creep into your mind. When you start to trust someone or something of this world to provide your meaning, your significance, or your self-worth, that's when insecurity will start to take hold in your heart.

There's nothing this world can offer and no relationship you can have, even with your wife, that can bear that burden of providing you with meaning and significance. There's no career, no house, no car, no material item that can bear that burden. However, if you have misplaced your trust in any of those to bear that burden for you, that's when you will start to hear the lies and negative thoughts in your mind.

When you start to feel insecure, and when you start to hear those thoughts, turn your focus towards me. Share what you're feeling with me. Trust that the Father is the solid rock that you can always count on. Recognize the insecurity as a lie from the enemy.

Trust that peace comes from knowing me, and from the eternal life that I bring, rather than anything here on earth. You are victorious with me. You are eternally secure with me.

Scriptures:

Jeremiah 17:7 "But blessed are those who trust in the Lord and have made the Lord their hope and confidence."

Isaiah 26:3-4 "You will keep in perfect peace all who trust in you, all whose thoughts are fixed on you! Trust in the Lord always, for the Lord God is the eternal Rock."

John 4:13-14 "Jesus replied, 'Anyone who drinks this water will soon become thirsty again. But those who drink the water I give them will never be thirsty again. It becomes a fresh, bubbling spring within them, giving them eternal life.'"

Questions: When you are feeling insecure, what is your mind focused on, instead of Jesus? How would it be different if you were able to give those insecurities to him?

THE BIG PICTURE

Even though I think I'm doing what I'm supposed to be doing, there are times when it's really difficult. I've heard from people things like, "when you do what you love, you'll never work a day in your life" or that "when your mission is aligned with who you are, your problems will go away". If those things are true, and I'm doing what I love and am in alignment with who I am, why do I still have these challenges?

Jesus: There will be times when you're on the right course, when you're doing the right thing, and when you're following your calling, yet you will still experience doubt, pain, and fear. Simply because you're doing what you were created to do does not mean you won't have trials, challenges, or periods when you question. This world has those struggles, there is no way of avoiding them. Even I did not avoid the struggles of this life.

I knew exactly what my mission was, from an early age. I knew exactly why I was walking the earth. I knew what the plan was. I knew what was going to happen. But that doesn't mean that I was looking forward to how it was going to end. There would be intense challenges (to put it mildly), and the pain of the cross was going to be overwhelming. It was going to be agonizing, excruciating, and humiliating.

However, even knowing that was coming, I stayed the course and kept my eyes on the bigger picture. I came to seek out and save all who are lost. I came to fulfill prophecy. I came to call people to repentance and to forgive those who ask for forgiveness. I came to lead everyone to God the Father.

There was testing, there were trials, there were times when it was nearly too much to bear. But I always looked towards the Father and always remembered the bigger picture. Every time things got intense, I relied on my relationship with the Father, and on the scriptures.

In your daily life, you must do the same. During your times of trial, keep your focus on the big picture. Remember your reason why for doing what you are doing. It's beyond the issue of the day, it's beyond the problem at work or at home, your life is to be lived with me and for the Father.

Scriptures:

Matthew 26:38-38 "He told them, 'My soul is crushed with grief to the point of death. Stay here and keep watch with me.' He went on a little farther and bowed with his face to the ground, praying, 'My Father! If it is possible, let this cup of suffering be taken away from me. Yet I want your will to be done, not mine."

John 3:16-17 "For this is how God loved the world: He gave his one and only Son, so that everyone who believes in him will not perish but have eternal life. God sent his Son into the world not to judge the world, but to save the world through him."

2 Corinthians 5:15 "He died for everyone so that those who receive his new life will no longer live for themselves. Instead, they will live for Christ, who died and was raised for them."

Questions: How do you stay on the path looking at the big picture, when doing what you know is the right thing? What ways do you refocus on Jesus, during your times of trial? What is your reason why for doing what you're doing?

A PROUD MAN

I have to admit that I want people to like me, and I want them to like my work. I can feel those wants sometimes leading me to being more prideful than I know I should be. How do I reconcile those wants with who you have called me to be?

Jesus: This is related to when we were talking about ego earlier. Just like ego is not automatically good or bad, neither is pride automatically good or bad. However, with that being said, pride is a major challenge for many men and does often end up on the bad side of the equation more than the good side.

But, there's nothing wrong with taking pride in a job well done. When you work hard and accomplish something great, you should be satisfied in what you have completed. Likewise, there's nothing wrong with you being proud for what someone you love has accomplished. Those are two times when pride is certainly understandable and not a problem.

It's the other kind of pride that you need to watch out for. And sadly, this is more common for most men. This is the pride of thinking that what you have done is all about you. This is the pride that comes from you feeling self-righteous or better than other people. This is the pride that has you taking the credit for something that was a gift from the Father. This is the pride that leads you to state that you have figured it all out and achieved everything all on your own.

That pride is something you must work to eliminate immediately. Your enemy uses that pride to make you think that you can do everything by yourself, and that what you can do alone is greater than anything you could do with me. Those lies are powerful as they strike directly in the heart of men.

You are to remain humble in your victories. You are to remember that all you achieve, both great and small, is a gift from God. You are to give thanks to the Father, with a gracious heart, for all that you accomplish. And when you do that, I'm proud of you!

Scriptures:

Galatians 6:4 "Pay careful attention to your own work, for then you will get the satisfaction of a job well done, and you won't need to compare yourself to anyone else."

James 4:6 And he gives grace generously. As the Scriptures say, 'God opposes the proud but gives grace to the humble.'"

Luke 18:14 "I tell you, this sinner, not the Pharisee, returned home justified before God. For those who exalt themselves will be humbled, and those who humble themselves will be exalted."

Proverbs 18-19 "Pride goes before destruction, and haughtiness before a fall. Better to live humble with the poor than to share plunder with the proud."

1 Corinthians 4:7 "For what gives you the right to make such a judgment? What do you have that God hasn't given you? And if everything you have is from God, why boast as though it were not a gift?"

Questions: Has your pride ever stopped you from accepting who Jesus is and that you need him in your life? Have you given yourself the credit for things that you know are gifts from God?

RELIGIOUS LEADERS

In the Bible, there is quite a bit written about your interactions and conflicts with religious leaders. Why was there so much conflict between you and them?

Jesus: Oh, how much I could say here! We could spend days talking about this single question. I had frequent trouble from religious leaders, and political leaders, when I was walking here on earth. The group of leaders I clashed with the most were the Pharisees, while another group of leaders I had conflict with was the Sadducees. The Sadducees were a political party that was in favor with the Roman government of the time.

The Pharisees were often men who felt they were better than others and looked down on anyone they didn't deem worthy. The Sadducees were often men who were only strict on the written law and they rejected the various traditions held by the Pharisees. Those two groups didn't really like one another that much, although they came together in their dislike of what I came to teach and show the world.

It's very important to remember that my conflicts with them were based on their hypocrisy and how they chose to act in their daily lives. Their purely external following of the law, so that everyone could see what they were doing, while their spiritual lives were empty, was a primary point of conflict. In addition, their arrogance in believing that they were more religious, and more deserving than other people, was also a conflict.

I came for all people, all men and all women. The religious leaders of the day were angry and confused that I would dine with people they deemed "unworthy". My mission, my love, my message is for all men and women. No matter their societal standing, no matter their culture, no matter their income, no matter their background, and no matter their religious training, I came for them. That, among so many other things, is what has led to much conflict between me and religious leaders.

I'm here for everyone who chooses me. I'm here for you.

Scriptures:

Matthew 23:27-28 "What sorrow awaits you teachers of religious law and you Pharisees. Hypocrites! For you are like whitewashed tombs – beautiful on the outside but filled on the inside with dead people's bones and all sorts of impurity. Outwardly you look like righteous people, but inwardly your hearts are filled with hypocrisy and lawlessness."

Mark 2:15-17 "But when the teachers of religious law who were Pharisees saw him eating with tax collectors and other sinners, they asked his disciples, 'Why does he eat with such scum?' When Jesus heard this, he told them, 'Healthy people don't need a doctor – sick people do. I have come to call not those who think they are righteous, but those who know they are sinners.'"

Questions: Do you ever find yourself thinking that you're better than someone else? Do you ever find yourself more concerned with someone following the church rules than following Jesus?

HONORING YOUR PARENTS

Over the years, I have spoken to many men who have strained or outright broken relationships between themselves and their mothers or fathers. In some cases, the relationship is entirely broken between the man and both his parents due to some trauma, abuse, or otherwise horrible situation that caused the relationship to end. In other cases, the man was abandoned by one, or both, of his parents. These men have heard that they are supposed to honor their parents, but how do they do that, when coming from such a situation?

Jesus: The pain that can fall onto a boy, from a parent, is unique; it's unlike any other pain that can happen. When that pain is in the form of abuse, of any sort, it certainly can fracture a relationship, and when that happens my heart breaks.

In this context, a situation with an abusive parent is very much like our conversation about forgiveness. What I mean by that is when you honor your parents, you're doing that more for you than you are for them. Holding onto the pain, the history, the hurt, and the resentment will never bring you peace, or contentment, or bring you closer to me or the Father.

Just as forgiveness does not mean that what happened in the past is now ok, honoring your parents, when coming from a difficult or painful situation, does not mean that what happened is now ok. Remember that justice is separate from forgiveness and justice is separate from honoring.

Honoring your mother and father is a commandment, not because it is easy, but because it's that important. And honoring helps you, for the life you are experiencing, and for your own heart.

For the man who is coming from such challenges, give that pain to me. Let me carry that burden for you. Choose to release that to me, so that you may grow in love for yourself and for those who gave you life.

For the man who has not dealt with abuse or trauma from a parent in the past, you're still given the commandment to honor your parents. For the man who has not experienced such a past, it's easy to forget this, in the busyness of life, but it should not be forgotten.

Every man is to honor his parents; in doing so he will experience peace and the Father will look on him with loving eyes.

Scriptures:

Exodus 20:12 "Honor your father and mother. Then you will live a long, full life in the land the Lord your God is giving you." Proverbs 23:25 "So give your father and mother joy! May she who gave you birth be happy."

2 Timothy 3:2 "For people will love only themselves and their money. They will be boastful and proud, scoffing at God, disobedient to their parents, and ungrateful. They will consider nothing sacred."

Questions: What do you do, to honor your parents? If you are coming to this section with such pain in your past, will you commit to giving that pain to Jesus, so that you may grow, love, and learn to honor your parents?

UNCOMFORTABLE TRUTH

We currently live in a culture where we're very concerned about what other people might think or say about what we might think or say. On the one hand, this is good, no one should ever be purposefully hurting others with their actions or words. But, on the other hand, it seems like people then end up never speaking what they are really thinking or feeling. How is it that you seem to always speak the truth, even when people get uncomfortable or might not want to hear what you have to say?

Jesus: When sharing with people, truths which are uncomfortable or that they don't want to hear, I often have to alter how I say what I say for each person. With some people I am very direct, because that's what their hearts need to hear. With other people, I'm gentler, still sharing the truth, but in a manner that allows that truth to pierce their hearts. The truth is always the truth, no matter how uncomfortable it might be. However, it does need to be delivered differently to different people at different times.

For example, most of the Pharisees were not looking to learn or to soften their hearts; rather they were only looking to trap me or find some legal way of getting rid of me. Knowing the law, as they did, required me to be much more direct in my rebuke. I would speak truth to them with a sharper tone, with more irony, wit, and sarcasm.

A different time I was talking with my friend Nicodemus, who was a respected teacher himself, but he was unsure of the things I came to share. He needed a softer response from me, not a harsh rebuke. In his case, a sharp tone would not have been effective when sharing the truth.

There were even times that I had to correct my own disciples, before they truly knew me, knew my mission, and knew my purpose on earth. For them I chose to correct and speak the truth in all different manners, sometimes short and direct, and sometimes longer with more teaching.

If I were to speak the same way, in the same manner, to all people about all issues, the message would frequently be lost. People would lose my commitment to love, would lose the point that I came to fulfill prophecies, and would lose the fact that I came to seek and save those who are lost.

Scriptures:

Luke 11:39 "Then the Lord said to him, 'You Pharisees are so careful to clean the outside of the cup and the dish, but inside you are filthy – full of greed and wickedness!"

John 3:10 "You are a respected Jewish teacher, and yet you don't understand these things?"

Matthew 8:25-26 "The disciples went and work him up, shouting, 'Lord, save us! We're going to drown!' Jesus responded, 'Why are you afraid? You have so little faith!' Then he got up and rebuked the wind and waves, and suddenly there was a great calm.

Questions: What times have you been afraid to say what you're thinking, for concern about how others will react? Have you ever felt the call to share the good news of Jesus, but held back due to what other people might think?

FEARLESS MAN

When I was a little boy, I had typical fears. Things like spiders or hornets would get me very worried, very quickly. Once I became a husband and a father, my fears changed, and once I had a few more years on me, my fears changed again. My fears shifted to things like a fear of not protecting my family, or of not mattering to anyone, or not making a difference in the world. How can I remove these fears from my life?

Jesus: There are elements of fear that are good and worth keeping in our lives, so to live truly without any fear of anything wouldn't be a healthy life. Fear of the consequences when you're about to make a bad decision, for example, is a healthy fear. Being afraid and respectfully retreating when you cross the path of a grizzly bear, is a healthy fear. The goal should not be to remove all fear from your life, rather to remove unhealthy fears.

Unhealthy fears cause you to be separated from me. Unhealthy fears cause you to withdrawal back from who you could become. Unhealthy fears cause you to feel paralyzed, nervous, anxious, and uncertain of your future.

That kind of fear is a lie, an attack from the enemy, designed to keep you afraid and disconnected from me. You already matter to the Father, as you were wonderfully created in his image. Remember, that before you were born, before your wife was born, before your children were born, they were already part of the Father's family.

You were not created with a spirit of fear, but instead you were created with a spirit of power, of love, and self-discipline. So bring your fears to me, share them with the Father in prayer. In your fears, you are never alone. In the darkest valleys of your life, you are never alone. I'm with you, and together there is victory over your fears.

Scriptures:

Psalm 23:4 "Even when I walk through the darkest valley, I will not be afraid, for you are close beside me. Your rod and your staff protect and comfort me."

2 Timothy 1:7 "For God has not given us a spirit of fear and timidity, but of power, love, and self-discipline."

1 John 4:17-18 "And as we live in God, our love grows more perfect. So we will not be afraid on the day of judgment, but we can face him with confidence because we live like Jesus here in this world. Such love has no fear, because perfect love expels all fear. If we are afraid, it is for fear of punishment, and this shows that we have not fully experienced his perfect love."

Luke 24:36-38 "And just as they were telling about it, Jesus himself was suddenly standing there among them. 'Peace be with you,' he said. But the whole group was startled and frightened, thinking they were seeing a ghost! 'Why are you frightened?' he asked. 'Why are your hearts filled with doubt?'"

Questions: How does holding onto your unhealthy fears impact your life? What fears have you not yet fully given over to Jesus?

BREAKING THE RULES

Sometimes it can feel like Christianity is all about rules. Do this. Don't do that. It can become stifling and take all the joy out of life. If all we are to do is follow a set of rules, well that isn't something that most men have any interest in as they have enough rules to follow already. Did you ever break any rules?

Jesus: Ha! Oh yes, I broke all sorts of rules in all sorts of ways. One of the reasons that so many of the Pharisees wanted to get rid of me was because I'm such a rule breaker! Of course, the rules that I break, are never really the point. The point was people missing the bigger picture, missing the reason I had come, missing the life beyond the rules.

When I healed a woman's back on the Sabbath, there were people more concerned about which day of the week that I had healed her, than they were about the fact that she was released from her sickness. Likewise, when I healed a man's hand on the Sabbath, again the Pharisees were so enraged that they plotted how to kill me. They could not even answer me when I asked if the law permitted good deeds on the Sabbath.

I would break other rules as well. One time I had been out walking and was very tired and thirsty. I came across a well where a Samaritan woman was and asked her for a drink. At the time this was breaking many rules. Jews did not talk with Samaritans, and a single Jewish man would never talk to a single Samaritan woman alone. That was some scandalous rule breaking for sure, and I was happy to do it, as it led to the bigger picture of who I was and why I came.

So even though I was breaking the rules, I knew why I was there, and because of our conversation, many Samaritans in that village came to know and believe in me. That is far more important to me than any rule about a Jewish man not talking with a Samaritan woman. I want everyone on earth to come to me and know me, and if I have to break some rules to make that happen, then so be it!

Scriptures:

Luke 13:14 "But the leader in charge of the synagogue was indignant that Jesus had healed her on the Sabbath day. 'There are six days of the week for working,' he said to the crowd. 'Come on those days to be healed, not on the Sabbath.'"

Mark 3:6 "At once the Pharisees went away and met with the supporters of Herod to plot how to kill Jesus."

John 4:9 "The woman was surprised, for Jews refuse to have anything to do with Samaritans. She said to Jesus, 'You are a Jew, and I am a Samaritan woman. Why are you asking me for a drink?'"

Matthew 9:10-11 "Later, Matthew invited Jesus and his disciples to his home as dinner guests, along with many tax collectors and other disreputable sinners. But when the Pharisees saw this, they asked his disciples, 'Why does your teacher eat with such scum?'"

Questions: What rules do you hold onto that you think Jesus might break, if it could bring more people to him? What will you do to bring more people to him?

JOY OF LIFE

Speaking of rules, some of the Christian men I know seem to be overly concerned with rules, disagreeing about people standing or kneeling in prayer, debating what kind of music should be in church, arguing over which version of the Bible to use, and on and on. These men seem to have very little joy in their lives, especially at church. Does the Christian life include joy?

Jesus: When men are consumed with those details or legalistic functions of church, they're losing sight of the joy that I want them to be filled with. That joy is to come from me, not from a rule within a church. In fact, one of the reasons for my teaching is so that men will experience my true joy. I want men to be overflowing with joy and sharing that joy with the world. I want men to be so filled with love and joy that others will seek them out to find out what they are doing differently.

An early moment of joy in my mission happened was when my disciples and I were invited to celebrate a wedding. Weddings are meant to be joyous occasions, and I did enjoy attending a great party. During this party, the supply of wine ran out, and my mother asked me to do something about it. This is when I turned water into enough wine, and really excellent tasting wine I should add, to keep the party going. As I was smiling and laughing along, it was a joy-filled evening for everyone.

For men who are lacking joy in their lives, they're looking in the wrong places. They may be looking to momentary events of fun, yet those will not fulfill the need for joy a man feels in his soul. True joy will only come through me, increasing faith, understanding the scriptures, and knowing the Father.

Think of it like this: imagine that I'm the vine and you're one of the branches. The branch is where the fruit is located, but that branch cannot survive without the vine. If you think of your joy as the fruit found on the branch, you can see that there will be no fruit, no joy, without a direct connection to me.

When you experience joy, with me, your heart and your spirit will be full. When you experience joy, with me, you will have strength to share. When you experience joy, with me, it fills my own heart and makes me smile.

Scriptures:

John 15:11 "I have told you these things so that you will be filled with my joy. Yes, your joy will overflow!"

John 2:7-10 "Jesus told the servants, 'Fill the jars with water.' When the jars had been filled, he said, 'Now dip some out, and take it to the master of ceremonies.' So the servants followed his instructions. When the master of ceremonies tasted the water that was now wine, not knowing where it had come from (though, of course, the servants knew), he called the bridegroom over. 'A host always serves the best wine first,' he said. 'Then, when everyone has had a lot to drink, he brings out the less expensive wine. But you have kept the best until now!'"

Proverbs 17:22 "A cheerful heart is good medicine, but a broken spirit saps a person's strength."

Questions: When you think of Jesus, can you picture him smiling, laughing, drinking wine at a wedding, and filled with joy? Where are you looking for joy in your life, right now?

NOT TOO FAST

Sometimes when I get an idea to do something, I just want to jump right in. I want to get to work. I want to create things. I want to see what happens next. And sometimes when I do that, things work out. But usually things turn into a disaster that needs fixing. I end up wasting time, wasting money, and wasting effort. Why does this happen, even when the things I'm trying to do are positive and to help other people?

Jesus: When you jump right into action, without taking time to plan, to prepare, and to pray, you're opening yourself up to challenge. Your enemy likes to use your enthusiasm and energy in a misplaced manner. Your enemy knows that if you're not prepared, it will be easier to knock you off your course.

It's understandable when you get excited about an opportunity, but you need to step back and pray about that opportunity. You have to listen and learn, in order to determine if that is in fact the direction you should be taking. Sometimes what looks like an opportunity is actually an obstacle to what your true calling is. Sometimes going too fast will cause you to end up much farther away from your calling than when you started.

If you were to start building a new house, without any idea if you could pay to complete the construction, people would rightfully question your decision to start. If you commanded an army, and you were to attack an opposing force that was twice the size, without first figuring out your path to victory, again people would rightfully question your decision to attack.

You do need to plan, you do need to prepare, and you do need to pray. Pray for wisdom over the decision that you are considering. Pray for guidance over the action you are about to take. Read the scriptures to discern the truth about your ideas. Be willing to patiently wait for the understanding you need to move closer to your calling.

Being a follower of mine doesn't mean you don't have to plan. Yes, the Father will provide your needs, but that doesn't mean you're given what you want. So, it's unwise for you to have no plan. Your part is to prepare, to plan, and to use the gifts and talents that the Father has graciously given you.

Scriptures:

Proverbs 21:5 "Good planning and hard work lead to prosperity, but hasty shortcuts lead to poverty."

Luke 14:28,31 "But don't begin until you count the cost. For who would begin construction of a building without first calculating the cost to see if there is enough money to finish it? Or what king would go to war against another king without first sitting down with his counselors to discuss whether his army of 10,000 could defeat the 20,000 soldiers marching against him?"

2 Peter 3:9 "The Lord isn't really being slow about his promise, as some people think. No, he is being patient for your sake. He does not want anyone to be destroyed, but wants everyone to repent." Proverbs 2:6 "For the Lord grants wisdom! From His mouth comes knowledge and understanding."

Questions: When you are about to start something new, how well do you plan, prepare, and pray about it? Do you read the Scriptures to identify truth in your ideas?

COMMON DENOMINATOR

One of the questions I get asked, especially by non-believers, is about Christians having problems. They want to know why someone who believes in you continues to have problems. Should someone who is your follower still have troubles?

Jesus: Such a question is based on the flawed premise of a trouble-free life for a Christian. That's a myth, with no basis in reality. One point I made very clear to my disciples was the fact, the fact, that they will have trials and sorrows while walking the earth. I directly told them that they were going to have trouble, period. And the exact same thing is true for all those who follow me today and for my disciples today.

The reality that all men who follow me will have trouble is one of the common denominators between them all. The types of trouble will change for men who follow me; for some it will be in their health, others in their finances, others will be discriminated against, others will be hated, others will be jailed, and others will even be murdered. So, while the type of trouble will be different, there will be trouble.

This trouble comes, as we talked about before, especially when the choice to follow me has been made. That decision makes the enemy take notice, and he wants to take you out. You're a threat to him, you're his target, and he will continue to attack you as you follow me. All who follow me have that in common.

Now the good news is that all who follow me can take heart in the truth that I have overcome the world. The troubles of the world and the attacks of the enemy are overcome, through me. There is no need for any man to try and solve all his problems on his own, because that's too overwhelming. You will not be spared trouble when you follow me, but you will be delivered from that trouble into freedom.

Always remember, during your times of trouble and your times of peace, that I am with you and together we achieve victory. Always remember that I love you. Always remember that the Father loves you.

Scriptures:

John 16:33 "I have told you all this so that you may have peace in me. Here on earth you will have many trials and sorrows. But take heart, because I have overcome the world."

Psalm 34:19 "The righteous person faces many troubles, but the Lord comes to the rescue each time."

Romans 8:35,37 "Can anything ever separate us from Christ's love? Does it mean he no longer loves us if we have trouble or calamity, or are persecuted, or hungry, or destitute, or in danger, or threatened with death? No, despite all these things, overwhelming victory is ours through Christ, who loves us."

Questions: Have you ever thought that your life would be without troubles, once you followed Jesus? How does knowing that he has overcome the world, on your behalf, help you through your challenges?

BEING A PROVIDER

I understand that you said earlier that man was created to work, but I know there are men reading this who cannot work, due to injury or illness, or who have made the choice to stay at home with their children. I know that being a provider is a strong driver of men, but how is a man a provider if he is not working?

Jesus: This is a complex question. The reason for the complexity is how current culture has defined the word provide. It has become synonymous with finances, or with earning an income. And while it certainly is important that a man is to provide financially for his family, that is not the limitation of what it means to provide.

A man is to work at providing leadership for and teaching to his family. He is to work at providing spiritual guidance to his family. He is to work at providing loving and willing sex for his wife. He is to work at providing an encouraging home for his children. He is to work at providing for himself to learn, grow, and deepen his relationship with me. He is to work on providing a plan for the future, together with his wife. He is to work at providing mentoring to others.

A man is to work on providing all these things, as if he is working directly for the Father. God smiles on a man who works hard to provide these things to himself and those he has been called to provide for.

You see, all of these are important for a man who works to provides, and the financial aspect is only one single piece of the providing puzzle. This is not to discount the important nature of financial provision, rather to highlight how much more there is to being a provider.

Lastly, a man is not to simply provide for the pursuit of his own interests, especially if the result of that pursuit is him not providing any of these areas for his family. When a man puts aside what he wants to do, in order to provide for his family, or when he makes the choice to take a job and do work, he would rather not do, he should know that choice, that action, is viewed in a favorable light by the Father. This is a man who is acting like a warrior provider, doing what he knows he must above his own personal interests.

Scriptures:

Colossians 3:23 "Work willingly at whatever you do, as though you were working for the Lord rather than for people."

Ephesians 5:25 "For husbands, this means love your wives, just as Christ loved the church. He gave up his life for her to make her holy and clean, washed by the cleansing of God's word."

1 Timothy 5:8 "But those who won't care for their relatives, especially those in their own household, have denied the true faith. Such people are worse than unbelievers."

Colossians 3:21 "Fathers, do not aggravate your children, or they will become discouraged."

Questions: In which areas are you doing an excellent job of providing for your family? In which areas do you need to work on being a better provider?

THE BENEFITS

There are times when I sit back and looked at the house my family lives in and I feel grateful, then there are other times I look at the exact same house and I feel like it's too much. How do I walk that line between appreciating the benefits of my work and having too much?

Jesus: There is nothing wrong with working hard and enjoying the benefits of your hard work. There are plenty of rich men in heaven, as being rich neither qualifies you nor disqualifies you from entering heaven and enjoying fellowship with the Father.

The question is not about gaining benefits from working hard, rather it's about why you might seek those benefits and if those benefits have become a false idol for you.

If you become so focused on what you might gain, it can be a direct line for that focus to become an idol trap. You can end up so entirely about what your personal benefit could be that you lose sight of the big picture and you start chasing the benefits to provide you meaning. That's when the benefits you seek have turned into an idol, and when those benefits have crossed the line.

You are to use your skills to work hard, in order to provide for you, for your family, and for those in need. When you do so, don't just add more to your own bank account, but give with a generous heart to those you're able to help. You will have a hard time buying coats for the homeless and purchasing food for a pantry when you have nothing in your bank account. It's your job to reach out, to find those who you can help, and to help them. Don't ask anyone else to do that on your behalf, you do it yourself.

The more important place where you do what to add to your bank account, so to speak, is your heavenly bank account. Focus on building your heavenly account more than any other. Focus on doing good work for the Father. Focus on teaching others about me and the freedom I offer.

Scriptures:

Matthew 6:19 "Don't store up treasures here on earth, where moths eat them and rust destroys them, and where thieves break in and steal. Store your treasures in heaven, where moths and rust cannot destroy, and thieves do not break in and steal. Wherever your treasure is, there the desires of your heart will also be."

Ecclesiastes 5:18-19 "Even so, I have noticed one thing, at least, that is good. It is good for people to eat, drink, and enjoy their work under the sun during the short life God has given them, and to accept their lot in life. And it is a good thing to receive wealth from God and the good health to enjoy it. To enjoy your work and accept your lot in life – this is indeed a gift from God.

Ephesians 4:28 "If you are a thief, quit stealing. Instead, use your hands for good hard work, and then give generously to others in need."

Ecclesiastes 3:13 "And people should eat and drink and enjoy the fruits of their labor, for these are gifts from God."

Questions: How will you add to your heavenly bank account today? How will you build your earthly account, so that you give generously to those in need?

GUARD YOUR HEART

I want to follow-up on your last answer. You mentioned guarding the hearts of our children. I've also heard you talk about guarding my own heart. What does that really mean? How, and why, should I be guarding my heart and my children's hearts?

Jesus: The heart of a man is a complex, dangerous, and glorious thing. The Father looks to your heart, when discerning what you believe and who you really are. The Father looks to your heart to identify your motives and reasons for doing what you choose to do. That alone is reason enough to protect your heart, and your children's hearts, but there's more.

Your heart is also a primary point of attack for your enemy. An enemy attack on your heart, or the hearts of your children, can change your outlook on life, it can change how you behave, it can change what you believe, it can change your actions, and it can change your future.

Your enemy knows that if he can get you to think or feel something in your heart, it can become a stronghold that is hard to break. Your enemy knows that your heart is vulnerable to the attack, which is why you must be constantly vigilant in guarding it.

One of the most important ways of guarding your heart is to be consciously aware of what you put into your heart. You must protect yourself, from what can enter your heart, on all fronts. This includes everything from the people you have around you, to what you read, what music you listen to, and what you see. Conversations, television, social media, websites, music, and movies are all places where you must actively guard your heart. Choose what you allow to openly influence your heart.

During your times of trial and difficulty, your heart is particularly susceptible to attack. This is often when the enemy puts a lie into your heart. When this happens, come to me. Share your difficult times with me, focus your eyes on the Father. I'm here to walk with you, to carry your burdens, to help you through the confusing times, and to give you rest.

Surround your heart with my love and choose to let me help you guard your heart.

Scriptures:

Proverbs 4:23 "Guard your heart above all else, for it determines the course of your life."

Matthew 11:28-29 "Then Jesus said, 'Come to me, all of you who are weary and carry heavy burdens, and I will give you rest. Take my yoke upon you. Let me teach you, because I am humble and gentle at heart, and you will find rest for your souls."

Romans 12:2 "Don't copy the behavior and customs of this world, but let God transform you into a new person by changing the way you think. Then you will learn to know God's will for you, which is good and pleasing and perfect."

Questions: In what ways have you noticed the enemy attacking your heart? Have you noticed that the attacks tend to coincide with your times of struggle? Do you now realize that is not a coincidence? How will you bring Jesus into your plan of guarding your heart?

WHY ME?

I've mentioned about how nervous I was writing this book, having this conversation with you. I openly share with people that I'm not a trained preacher, I've not attended seminary school, and I do not have any formal religious training. I constantly have to fight back the feeling that I'm just a regular guy, and not worthy of writing this book. I often have to counter those kinds of thoughts, and I'm sure many other guys have the same, in their own lives. So, for myself, and those who have felt this same thing, I guess the question is why me to take on a project like this?

Jesus: I love this question, I really do. Because the truth is that this question gets right to the heart of such an important issue and is related to what we've talked about earlier. The world has convinced many people that only those who have the correct diploma on the wall can lead others to me. The world has convinced many people that only those who wear the correct robes or say the correct prayers at the correct times can lead others to me.

When the reality is that I have called everyone to do that. You will never find even one line of scripture about me saying that only certain people are allowed to teach the word or lead others to me. In fact, this was at the core of many of my challenges with the Pharisees, that they felt they were the only ones who could teach the law.

All throughout history, the Father has used regular guys to do his work. He was alongside Gideon, rescuing Israel when no one thought that would happen. He was alongside David, who defeated Goliath, when no one thought that would happen.

One of the reasons that I so love this is because it allows me to repeat the point that I have called every single man and woman. I have called all. I have called everyone. I have called you. No matter how small you might feel, no matter how low you might feel, no matter what you think your social standing is, I have called you. And when I see you answer that call, it makes my heart sing with joy!

Scriptures:

Ephesians 3:8 "Though I am the least deserving of all God's people, he graciously gave me the privilege of telling the Gentiles about the endless treasures available to them in Christ."

Judges 6:15-16 "'But Lord,' Gideon replied, 'how can I rescue Israel? My clan is the weakest in the whole tribe of Manasseh, and I am the least in my entire family!' The Lord said to him, 'I will be with you. And you will destroy the Midianites as if you were fighting against one man.'"

1 Samuel 17:32-33 "'Don't worry about this Philistine,' David told Saul. 'I'll go fight him!' 'Don't be ridiculous!' Saul replied. 'There's no way you can fight this Philistine and possibly win! You're only a boy, and he's been a man of war since his youth.'"

Questions: Have you ever felt a calling to do something for Jesus, but held back because you were wondering, why me? Knowing that Jesus will be filled with joy to see you take action on that calling, what will you now do differently?

SHINING BRIGHT

I have to admit that there are plenty of times when I see something happening, something I know isn't right, and I don't speak up. I end up more concerned about what other people might think of me than what you might think of me. I find it easier to just be quiet and not rock the boat. How do I know when I'm supposed to speak up and when I'm supposed to remain quiet?

Jesus: When you're in a pitch-black cave, a single candle can illuminate your way. When you're in a darkened room, a single light can brighten the entire space. Light is the one thing that can pierce and eliminate darkness. Likewise, truth is the one thing that can overthrow and destroy lies.

I am the light of this world. I am the one to bring the truth which defeats darkness and lies.

You cannot live in the light and in the darkness as the same time. You have to make a choice, you have to choose to either live in, and love, the light, or live in darkness and hate the light. And men who have made the decision to follow me, are men who have made the decision to live in the light.

Such men are obligated to shine their own lights into all areas of darkness in their lives, all the time. The truth is the truth, all the time. The light is the light, all the time.

It makes no sense for you to purchase a beautiful light for that darkened room, and then cover that light. That renders the light useless in that room. Instead, that light is to shine bright, forcing the darkness to retreat, and providing light to everyone in the room.

It's not easy to be that light when you're of the world. The enemy's attack on men of the world leads to a world filled with lies and darkness. This means that when you shine your light, you need to be prepared for the darkness to try and destroy your light. Be prepared for the lies and attacks to come at you strong, because the enemy hates it when you are a light shining brightly in the darkness.

However, seeing you be that light, seeing you shine bright, gives me incredible joy. Seeing you speak the truth in the shadows, no matter the situation, makes me proud of you, and makes the Father smile upon you. Be the man who shines bright in the darkness.

Scriptures:

John 8:12 "Jesus spoke to the people once more and said, 'I am the light of the world. If you follow me, you won't have to walk in darkness, because you will have the light that leads to life."

Ephesians 5:8-9 "For once you were full of darkness, but now you have light from the Lord. So live as people of light! For this light within you produces only what is good and right and true."

Matthew 5:16 "In the same way, let your good deeds shine out for all to see, so that everyone will praise your heavenly Father."

Questions: How do you shine, as a bright light, within your family? How do you shine, as a bright light, within your career or community? What areas of darkness do you feel called to shine a light on?

ONE AT A TIME

The church that I normally attend is large, with thousands of people, spread over multiple locations attending weekly. In a church that big, it can feel like the service is about the entire community, and not very personalized to any one in attendance. That's understandable, and the church does great things, so I'm heading in a different direction here. I'm wondering, even in a big group like that, do you build relationships with each person, or are you building the relationship between yourself and the entire church as a whole?

Jesus: No matter how big, or how small, a church happens to be, the relationship is always made one person at a time. I connect with each man, each woman, and each child, individually. It doesn't matter if there are three people or three thousand, I'm interested in every single person.

All ministry, whether we're talking about me and what I do, or you and what you do, it's all done through one single connection at a time. Every individual man who reads our conversation here is individually called to follow me and called to create disciples. He will create those disciples through one interaction at a time.

My compassion and caring are uniquely for you, because your walk is uniquely yours. I want you to bring me into the story of your life. I want you to share your peaks and your valleys with me. I want you to build a relationship with me, as the man who will always be with you.

There are multiple examples of me teaching entire crowds, and yet I still reached out to individuals in order to either talk with them one-on-one, or to heal them one at a time. No matter how many people were crowding around me, I would notice and attend to someone who called to me.

The same exact thing continues today. Right now, I'm connected with you. I'm listening to your prayers, I'm concerned about your heart. I'm standing beside you, and I'm lifting you during your times of challenge. I want to build a victorious relationship with you, individually.

Scriptures:

John 5:3,5-6 "Crowds of sick people – blind, lame, or paralyzed – lay on the porches. One of the men lying there had been sick for thirty-eight years. When Jesus saw him and knew he had been ill for a long time, he asked him, 'Would you like to get well?'"

Mark 7:32-33 "A deaf man with a speech impediment was brought to him, and the people begged Jesus to lay his hands on the man to heal him. Jesus led him away from the crowd so they could be alone..."

Luke 15:6-7 "When he arrives, he will call together his friends and neighbors, saying, 'Rejoice with me because I have found my lost sheep.' In the same way, there is more joy in heaven over one lost sinner who repents and returns to God than over ninety-nine others who are righteous and haven't strayed away!"

Questions: Do you realize that, no matter how many people you have around you, Jesus wants to build a relationship with you, individually? Who are some people that you could have one-on-one conversations with to share the good news of Jesus?

WAITING

Although I'm a patient man, I also have the desire to have the answers now, to solve the problem immediately, and to not have to wait for anything. Yes, it can get messy inside my head with these two competing thoughts doing battle. At times waiting for an answer to my prayers makes me feel exhausted and wondering if the thing I'm waiting for will ever happen. Why do we often have to wait so long to receive an answer to our prayers?

Jesus: History is filled with great men who had to wait, sometimes waiting so long that they never saw the fruits of their own efforts. Joseph was imprisoned for over ten years. David was on the run from Saul for years. Moses was wandering the desert for forty years. Paul was repeatedly put into a prison, waiting to be released. Those men certainly had to wait.

Even I waited to begin my mission here on earth. For the first thirty years of my life, I was not constantly teaching and spreading the news about the Father, who I was, or why I was here. I was waiting until the time the Father had planned for me.

I've also been directly accused of taking too long myself. When I was coming to heal my good friend Lazarus, he had already died by the time I arrived. What those who accused me didn't realize, right then, was that I wasn't working according to their timeline. I was working according to the Father's timeline. When I healed Lazarus, and when he rose from his bed, only then did they begin to understand.

In terms of waiting to receive an answer to a prayer, don't confuse not getting the answer you want for not getting an answer. Sometimes the answer is yes, but often the answer is going to be no, and other times the answer is going to be not now. An answer of no, or an answer of not right now, is still an answer.

Use your times of waiting to examine your heart, examine your intentions, and to increase your faith. Use your times of waiting to refocus on the Father. Like some of the other great men to walk the earth, the times you spend waiting can become powerful moments in your life when you transform yourself into someone even greater than before.

Scriptures:

John 11:17,21 "When Jesus arrived at Bethany, he was told that Lazarus had already been in his grave for four days. Martha said to Jesus, 'Lord, if only you had been here, my brother would not have died.'"

Psalm 27:14 "Wait patiently for the Lord. Be brave and courageous. Yes, wait patiently for the Lord."

Deuteronomy 8:2 "Remember how the Lord your God led you through the wilderness for these forty years, humbling you and testing you to prove your character, and to find out whether or not you would obey his commands."

Questions: How can you use the times you are waiting to increase your faith? In what ways does waiting for a prayer to be answered transform you into someone greater than before?

OUTCASTS

I've attended a few religious gatherings, over the years, that made me feel uncomfortable. The reason was that everyone was pretending to be perfect, but there was an underlying judgment and criticism beneath every smile. These were not inviting places, and I cannot imagine what someone new to the faith would take away from such a gathering. There is a perception that Christianity is only for those who are already perfect and who look down on others. Is there are place for people who aren't perfect to come to faith with you?

Jesus: Earlier I mentioned how so many of my conflicts were with the Pharisees and other religious leaders. These were leaders who were very strict on the rules of the day, and on judging anyone they deemed unworthy. While the word Pharisee may be old for your culture, there are many of them walking around today. And despite my attempts to teach them, many choose to not listen and choose to not see what I offer.

The men who were my original disciples were certainly not perfect, as I've spoken about before. Some of these men were educated, but others were not. People were amazed by what my disciples could teach and what they could accomplish. I was friends with fishermen, craftsmen, and even tax collectors. And let me tell you that being friends with a tax collector back then was not looked on with accepting eyes. I wanted men with all sorts of personalities, all sorts of temperaments, all sorts of backgrounds, and all sorts of futures ahead of them.

It makes me sad when people get so overly focused on the rules that they miss the big picture. For example, one time I was having a meal and the host was offended that I didn't properly wash my hands. This man was far more concerned about what happened on the outside, than what was happening within his heart and in his soul.

I did not come just to talk and teach to those who were already doing well. I came for all, and that included tax collectors, prostitutes, lepers, and all the other outcasts and sinners of society. I have come to seek and save those who are lost. I have come for you.

Scriptures:

Acts 4:13 "The members of the council were amazed when they saw the boldness of Peter and John, for they could see that they were ordinary men with no special training in the Scriptures. They also recognized them as men who had been with Jesus."

Matthew 9:10-12 "Later, Matthew invited Jesus and his disciples to his home as dinner guests, along with many tax collectors and other disreputable sinners. But when the Pharisees saw this, they asked his disciples, 'Why does your teacher eat with such scum?' When Jesus hear this, he said, 'Healthy people don't need a doctor – sick people do.'"

Questions: How do you ensure that others feel welcomed at churches or events where you are present? Knowing that Jesus came for all, how do you remember to never look down on someone?

TOO FAR GONE

I just had a related thought on the prior question that I want to follow-up with. You said that you have come for everyone, that you are here to seek and save sinners. But, is it possible for someone to be too far gone for them to come to you? Can someone have made so many mistakes, sinned so much, and done so many bad things, that they are not to come to you?

Jesus: No matter how far someone has fallen, they can choose to come to me. No matter what things a person has done in their past, they can choose to come to me. No matter what mistakes someone has made, they can choose to come to me.

It's a lie of the enemy that a man can be too far gone to have a relationship with me, or to know the Father, or to embrace the life, victory, and freedom that I offer. No man is too far gone, and I mean that with all seriousness. Every man can return to me.

Perhaps the best example of this is Paul, who wrote much of what you know as the New Testament. Before he was commonly known as Paul he was known as Saul the Persecutor. When he was Saul, a great man who was following me named Stephen was killed by a mob. Not only was Saul present at the time, but directly consented in the death of Stephen.

Saul then went on a rampage, trying to wipe out any remnant of my teaching or my influence. He destroyed churches. He imprisoned men and women. He was consenting to the death of many. If there was ever a man who was too far gone, it would have been him. But, he wasn't too far gone.

When he was on the way to Damascus, I came to him and talked with him. I explained what he must do, and after three days he was baptized and regained his strength. Though his encounter with me, his entire mission and world changed. Instead of persecuting those who sought me, he made the choice to become a man who would lead people to me.

If I can use Saul/Paul for the glory of my Father's Kingdom, I can certainly pursue you! If you feel like you are too far gone, know that's a lie. I'm here, right now, waiting for you with a smile and open arms.

Scriptures:

Acts 8:3 "But Saul was going everywhere to destroy the church. He went from house to house, dragging out both men and women to throw them into prison."

Luke 19:10 "For the Son of Man came to seek and save those who are lost."

Acts 9:20-21 "And immediately he began preaching about Jesus in the synagogues, saying, 'He is indeed the Son of God!' All who heard him were amazed. 'Isn't this the same man who caused such devastation among Jesus' followers in Jerusalem?' they asked. 'And didn't he come here to arrest them and take them in chains to the leading priests?'"

Questions: Have you ever felt like you have made such a major mistake, or sinned so much that Jesus would never embrace you? How do you feel knowing that, whatever you have done in your past, Jesus is waiting for you, right now, with open arms?

HIDING FROM HIM

When I've messed up, sometimes I want to just hide my mistake, pretend no one will ever know, and try to can keep it all to myself. I must admit that sometimes I hope that you'll not see what I've done, and that maybe I can hide that from both you and God. Why is it foolish to try and hide what I've done, and what should I do instead?

Jesus: The reason this is a foolish idea is the simple truth that it is impossible to hide from the Father. There is not a single place you could go and be hidden from him. Before answering what you should do instead, I want you to think about this idea of hiding from God in a different way.

You tend to think about this as if you're physically moving from one place to another, like Jonah trying to take a boat and escape from the work God had called him to. However, there are other ways, beyond running, that you might be attempting to hide from God and from your calling.

One example is in your career. You can get so "busy" in your career, under the illusion that you're doing all this work to provide for your family. And yes, of course you need to provide, but not when it's done as a means of hiding from the calling you were given.

Another example is in your family. As much as I love the passion you have for your own family, when you get so "busy" with your family activities that you're not following the calling you were given, that is a method of trying to hide from the Father.

In other words, you can try to build these hideouts, where you don't have enough time for God, and you are trying to ignore the calling that you feel on your heart. But, you cannot hide from the Father. Instead of trying to hide, you need to bring all your thoughts and concerns to me. Share with me what's going on in your life, and how you're feeling about the calling you've been given.

Don't hide from your calling, run towards it!

Scriptures:

Jonah 1:3 "But Jonah got up and went in the opposite direction to get away from the Lord. He went down to the port of Joppa, where he found a ship leaving for Tarshish. He bought a ticket and went on board, hoping to escape from the Lord by sailing to Tarshish.

Jeremiah 23:24 "'Can anyone hide from me in a secret place? Am I not everywhere in all the heavens and the earth?' says the Lord."

Hebrews 4:12-13 "For the word of God is alive and powerful. It is sharper than the sharpest two-edged sword, cutting between soul and spirit, between joint and marrow. It exposes our innermost thoughts and desires. Nothing in all creation is hidden from God. Everything is naked and exposed before his eyes, and he is the one to whom we are accountable."

Questions: Have you ever tried to hide something from God? What do you think would happen if you openly shared your thoughts with him instead? What is something you know you have been called to do, but have been hiding so that you wouldn't do it?

NOT ENOUGH

During the times of my life when things have been going well, I've noticed that I still end up concerned about the future, about what might happen next, and about having enough for those I love and care for. During the times that have been very hard, I end up concerned that, no matter what I do, I'll never have enough for those same people. How do I break out of that mindset?

Jesus: The scarcity mindset, of never having enough, is one that can trap everyone. It's a mindset that limits your belief and limits your faith. It's a mindset that's usually based on fear. It's a mindset that you need to work to change and is one that men have struggled with for thousands of years.

A great example of this was with my own disciples. I had been teaching and leading a crowd of thousands. It was getting late in the day, and everyone was getting tired and hungry. I told my disciples to feed the crowd, but they didn't see enough to go around. They were looking at the situation through the perspective of a scarcity mindset and not having enough.

Even as I stood among them, they couldn't see the truth. The heat of the moment took over, and they didn't recognize the abundance that I offer. So, I asked them to give me what they could find, and then I multiplied what they brought to me to feed the entire crowd. Not only that, I provided so much that we had full baskets of leftovers.

When you're looking at your life with a scarcity mindset, like my disciples were, you'll feel pulled down by your fears and your anxieties over the future. When you're looking at your life with an abundant mindset, you'll feel lifted and encouraged in all situations.

I'm here to provide a life filled with abundance. With that truth, it's important for you to realize that doesn't mean you'll have all your material desires met with abundance. Because, abundance isn't found in having all the things you want; rather it's in being close to me and the Father, and in trusting him to provide what you need, but not necessarily what you want. Every day I'm here to provide you with an abundance of the everlasting bread, water, and life that you need.

Scriptures:

Matthew 14:19-20 "Then he told the people to sit down on the grass. Jesus took the five loaves and two fish, looked up towards heaven, and blessed them. Then, breaking the loaves into pieces, he gave the bread to the disciples, who distributed it to the people. They all ate as much as they wanted, and afterward, the disciples picked up twelve baskets of leftovers."

John 6:35 "Jesus replied, 'I am the bread of life. Whoever comes to me will never be hungry again. Whoever believes in me will never be thirsty.'"

Romans 8:31 "What shall we say about such wonderful things as these? If God is for us, who can ever be against us?"

Questions: When you are challenged with a scarcity mindset, do you come to Jesus with your challenges, or try to figure it out all on your own? In what ways can you let go of your desire to control and instead allow Jesus to provide you with abundance?

FEAR NOT

I want to follow-up on the question about being fearless I asked you earlier. You talked about how men are created with a spirit of power, of love, and self-discipline. I appreciate that and will do my best to remember that. However, even as I pray about my fears, I notice that sometimes they come back. Why is fear such a powerful force in my mind, how do I defend myself against my fearful thoughts?

Jesus: Fear is a primary tool of the enemy, as I shared earlier. He lies to you about what might happen, so that you would be afraid. He lies to you about what might not happen, so that you would be afraid. He lies over and over, to ramp up your level of uncertainty, doubt, and fear.

The lies he whispers into your mind are designed to make you fearful. He hopes that his lies will cause you to pull back, to not shine your light, to not live in the truth, to remain in the darkness, and to never become the man you were created to become. But that fear is a lie, those are all lies.

Countering those lies is why I talk about so often is for my followers not to be held captive by fear. As I told them in the past, I tell you know: take heart, have courage, and do not fear what could come next. And most of all, to have faith. Because your faith is the direct counter-response to the lies of fear. Your faith is what makes fear dissolve away.

One time, when I was out in a boat with the guys, a great storm had come up while I was sleeping. The men became consumed with fear, as they had forgotten that I was with them. So they woke me up, panicked and full of fear about what might happen. What did happen was quite the surprise to them.

I rebuked the storm so that we would be on still waters again. As I calmed the storm, I gave the guys a quick reminder that they should not be afraid, and that they needed to increase their faith. These men had seen what I had done, but did not yet fully believe who I was, their faith was not yet to that level.

Your level of faith in who I am, your level of awareness that the Father is in control, that is your defense to lies of fear. Even during your toughest storm, have faith and fear not.

Scriptures:

Luke 8:24-25 "The disciples went and work him up, shouting, 'Master, Master, we're going to drown!' When Jesus woke up, he rebuked the wind and the raging waves. Suddenly the storm stopped and all was calm. Then he asked them, 'Where is your faith?' The disciples were terrified and amazed. 'Who is this man?' they asked each other. 'When he gives a command, even the wind and waves obey him!'"

Isaiah 41:10 "Don't be afraid, for I am with you. Don't be discouraged, for I am your God. I will strengthen you and help you. I will hold you up with my victorious right hand."

2 Timothy 1:7 "For God has not given us a spirit of fear and timidity, but of power, love, and self-discipline."

Questions: How does your level of faith in Jesus impact your level of fear in the world? What storms in your life have you called on Jesus to rebuke, for you? Do you have faith that he can?

COURAGE

Courage is one of those words that inspires men. We want to be men of courage. We want to show courage, to be courageous. For most men, at least in Western societies, we live in places that require little courage, at least the way most men think about courage. How is a man to be courageous, when he feels like there is nothing in his life that requires much courage?

Jesus: Part of the problem with how men think of courage is that they tend to limit it in such a way as you have described. However, a courageous man goes well beyond being a soldier, or police officer, or firefighter. Those are courageous careers, without question, however your career choice is not the limitation of where you live a life of courage.

In many parts of the world today, simply professing your faith in me is enough to have you tortured or killed. A man who will stand up and claim that he knows me and follows me is showing a powerful form of courage, and the Father always sees when that happens.

In other parts of the world today, standing up for me can cause a man to lose his career or his business. If you're in such a situation and you're clear in your love for me, that courage causes me great joy!

Other forms of courage include you being strong enough to forgive those who have hurt you. Or for you to finally forgive yourself. Or for you to honor his parents, even if you feel like they don't deserve it. Or for you to have a difficult conversation with a friend or one of your kids. Those all take great courage.

Another form of courage, that many men avoid, is when you take action to improve your marriage. When you swallow your pride, and do the work you need to do, that takes courage.

When you're feeling like you lack the courage you need, remember where your courage comes from. The Father and I will fill you with the spirit and courage you need, for whatever is facing you. When you do the right thing, when you stand up and profess your faith in me, I'm proud of you and filled with joy. And when the Father sees you courageously stand up for him, he smiles on you.

Scriptures:

Psalm 31:24 "Be strong, and let your heart take courage, all you who wait for the Lord!"

2 Chronicles 32:7-8 "Be strong and courageous. Do not be afraid or dismayed before the king of Assyria and all the horde that is with him, for there are more with us than with him. With him is an army of flesh, but with us is the Lord of God, to help us and fight our battles."

Matthew 24:9 "Then they will deliver you up to tribulation and put you to death, and you will be hated by all nations for my name's sake."

Acts 4:29 "And now Lord, look upon their threats and grant to your servants to continue to speak your word with all boldness."

Questions: Has there ever been a time when you wanted to profess your faith in Jesus, but you held back out of concern for what other people might think? How can you show courage in improving the relationship with your wife?

EARN MY WAY

The idea that you are the only way into heaven is something that bothers lots of men. How come I can't just do good things, be a good person, and earn my way into heaven?

Jesus: This is one of those uncomfortable truths we talked about earlier, and the question itself is based on a misunderstanding about the nature of goodness in people. I can best answer this by telling you about a situation that happened to me.

I was leaving town, with my disciples, and a young man came up to me. This young man was wealthy, and he wanted to know what he had to do, to get into heaven.

Knowing where the conversation would end up, I replied by saying that he had to live the ten commandments at all times of his life. He claimed that he had always done so, even when he was young. However, I could see in him that he was currently clinging to a very strong idol. He had created a false god of wealth and self-sufficiency, and he had placed that idol higher than the Father.

To challenge him, I told him that he was to give away all of his wealth to the poor and follow me. But because his wealth had become an idol to him, he was unable to do this, and he walked away in sorrow. It wasn't the fact that he had wealth, it was the fact that his wealth had become an idol, and that idol had corrupted his own heart.

You see the challenge of earning your way into heaven is found within the heart of a man, not in his outward appearance or external actions. Because of that, the idea of being good enough itself is a flawed premise.

It is from within the heart where greed, pride, lust, adultery, stealing, murder and so on all originate. A man who acts perfectly on the outside may be hiding a heart filled with hatred, anger, greed, and contempt for his fellow man.

Your salvation is not based on your own goodness, because it's impossible for a man to be truly good enough, in his heart. Only God is good enough. Your salvation is a gift, from the Father, and through me, which I freely offer to all who choose to have faith and follow me.

Scriptures:

Mark 7:14-15 "Then Jesus called to the crowd to come and hear. 'All of you listen,' he said, 'and try to understand. It's not what goes into your body that defiles you; you are defiled by what comes from your heart.'"

Mark 10:17-18 "And as he was setting out on his journey, a man ran up and knelt before him and asked him, 'Good Teacher, what must I do to inherit eternal life?' And Jesus said to him, 'Why do you call me good? No one is good except God alone.'"

Ephesians 2:8-9 "God saved you by his grace when you believed. And you can't take credit for this; it is a gift from God. Salvation is not a reward for the good things we have done, so none of us can boast about it."

Questions: Have you ever thought you could just be good enough and get into heaven, without faith or following Jesus? Can you see how the problem of being good enough is found within your heart, and not within your actions?

CALLING YOU

From the men I know, one of the most profound changes in their lives comes when they feel the calling to do more. For some, they even set out on all new career paths. For others, they create new organizations serving others. And for others, they travel and help people out all over the world. What does it mean to be called in this way? Will you eventually call all men?

Jesus: When a man feels a calling, that's indeed a powerful moment in his life. It will often feel like the answer to a lifelong prayer, and it's important that he recognize that moment. But keep in mind that knowing what your calling is and acting upon that calling are two different things.

You, like every other man, have a purpose to play in your life; and your calling will often be directly connected to your purpose. It's important to know that your purpose and calling might not be what, where, or when you expect it to be.

It's also important to know that a man's calling does not necessarily mean it will be tied to his church. Not every man will be called to function as a pastor, or go on a mission trip to another continent, or anything like that. Some men will be called to serve as a brightly shining light in the darkness of their careers or business communities. Some men will be called to lead their families with love through difficult times they never expected to experience.

All men, not just professional religious leaders, will be called at some point in their lives. And when that call comes, it's up to each man to answer the call. When you feel the call, know that it's from the Father inviting you into the next chapter of your life's story.

As a man who follows me, will you receive a call from the Father? Yes, you will. Will it come to you when, and how, you want it? Probably not. Will it be time for you to answer the call, to live in freedom, experience victory, serve others with love, and follow the calling that you have been given? Yes, you know that it is. Will the Father smile on you when he sees you answer his call? Without question!

Scriptures:

Romans 8:28 "And we know that God causes everything to work together for the good of those who love God and are called according to his purpose for them."

2 Timothy 1:9 "For God saved us and called us to live a holy life. He did this, not because we deserved it, but because that was his plan from before the beginning of time – to show us his grace through Christ Jesus."

Matthew 9:13 "Then he added, 'Now go and learn the meaning of this Scripture: 'I want you to show mercy, not offer sacrifices.' For I have come to call not those who think they are righteous, but those who know they are sinners.'"

Galatians 5:13 "For you have been called to live in freedom, my brothers and sisters. But don't use your freedom to satisfy your sinful nature. Instead, use your freedom to serve one another in love."

Questions: Have you ever assumed that to be called by God meant you had to go into a religious profession or on a mission trip or similar? How has God called you to act, in your career and your family? Are you ignoring the call, because it is easier to remain where you are?

TRAINING FOR THE LONG RUN

There are definitely times when I feel exhausted from trying so hard; trying when my problems, struggles, challenges, and trials seem overwhelming. I have to remind myself that my current situation is only temporary and that I need to keep my eyes on the big picture. But, sometimes it's really hard to do that, at least for me. How do I persevere through those times?

Jesus: First of all, no matter what situation you find yourself in, know that you're not alone. I'm always with you. We've talked about staying in the fight, and this is a continuation of that part of our conversation.

You persevere by remaining focused on what I've taught. You persevere by remembering that your trails are temporary. You persevere by learning in every situation and applying what you've learned.

Think about what athletes normally train for. An athlete here on earth will prepare and train to run a race, a race where the prize will soon fade away and be forgotten. When you're my follower however, you're training and racing for a prize that remains eternal; a prize that will never fade away.

When you stand up and resist the temptations in front of you, including the temptation to quit your calling, you'll be blessed by the Father. It makes me proud when I see you push back on the testing and the temptation. I'm honored when I see you deepen your faith through your trials.

As you're facing those trials, it's important to fall back on your faith and the Scriptures to persevere. You need to develop endurance during these times so that you're able to build your strength and hope. When I was being tested, when the enemy was attacking me, I would use the scriptures as a big part of my response and I would pray to the Father.

When you are being tested, do the same as me when I was tested. Use the scriptures to endure. Share what you're going through with me. Bring your concerns and your needs to the Father, in prayer. Your perseverance and your endurance are all part of your training. And remember, you're training not for a prize that will fade away, but a prize that is eternal. You're training for the long run.

Scriptures:

James 1:12 "God blesses those who patiently endure testing and temptation. Afterward they will receive the crown of life that God has promised to those who love him."

1 Corinthians 9:27 "I discipline my body like an athlete, training it to do what it should. Otherwise, I fear that after preaching to others I myself might be disqualified."

Romans 5:3-4 "We can rejoice, too, when we run into problems and trials, for we know that they help us develop endurance. And endurance develops strength of character, and character strengthens our confident hope of salvation."

Questions: Are you more focused on winning an earthly prize that will fade away, or the eternal prize? How are you training and building your endurance and your perseverance?

FINISH WELL

Starting projects is so much fun for me, the energy and enthusiasm of something new is exciting, and I find it easy to start a project. After that, however, that's where the real work comes into the equation, and sometimes I don't do well in finishing projects, which frustrates me. So, with whatever I have going on in my life, how do I finish well?

Jesus: Sometimes, when you get stuck on a project and have difficulty finishing it, you've forgotten your reason why you started it in the first place. Other times, you didn't plan out what the project was really about or really required. You might get busy with things, and the project becomes another chore, another item on your to-do list. When you first started, you were feeling empowered by the excitement and the reason you were doing the project, to begin with.

If you've lost that reason why, you will find yourself in the situation where projects do not get completed, because other projects have taken precedence in your life. Be careful in these times, as it's possible that your enemy is working to make your life very busy, so that you let your dream slip away or you let your calling fall down on your priority list or forget about it entirely.

No matter what the project is, no matter what calling you feel, you can accomplish it when you bring me into your life. But remember, just because you have invited me into your life and your project, as you should, don't forget that you still have to do the work. And lots of times there will be hard work. Big, and great, projects aren't going to finish themselves, and if they were easy you would already have done them. You have to do the work.

So if you're struggling to finish, check your plan, remember your why, and focus time about the project every day in prayer. Ask the Father if this is the project for you, because sometimes it isn't and that's the reason for the challenge of finishing, and believe that together we can accomplish anything.

Then, when you do finish that project, you'll experience a great sense of accomplishment and achievement. You are to take the time to enjoy what you've done. And I'll do the same!

Scriptures:

2 Timothy 4:7-8 "I have fought the good fight, I have finished the race, and I have remained faithful."

Acts 20:24 "But my life is worth nothing to me unless I use it for finishing the work assigned me by the Lord Jesus – the work of telling others the Good News about the wonderful grace of God."

2 Corinthians 8:10-11 "Here is my advice: It would be good for you to finish what you started a year ago. Last year you were the first who wanted to give, and you were the first to begin doing it. Now you should finish what you started. Let the eagerness you showed in the beginning be matched now by your giving."

Philippians 4:13 "For I can do everything through Christ, who gives me strength."

Questions: What project have you started that you know you must finish? What was your reason why for starting? How can you include Jesus in your project plans?

THE WARRIOR

The Bible is filled with stories of how God uses warrior men on his behalf. I must admit that the idea of being called to be a Christian warrior appeals to me, even when I don't feel like one. I also know that's up to Him and not me, but I want to be prepared. So how should I prepare to become a Christian warrior?

Jesus: There is a warrior to be found in the heart of every man, even if that warrior has long been hibernating. Now clearly not every man is going to head off to the literal battlefield and face enemy soldiers. However every man is going to find himself in the fight, as we've discussed.

As a man who follows me, you're part of my army. I realize that some today may choose to take offense at such a statement, but that doesn't change the truth of what I'm saying. You are at war, you are in the fight, and you are in the middle of the greatest battle of all time, right now.

As a warrior, you must train for the fight, and you must learn to use the weapons that have been created for you. When I was under assault, I continued to use the scriptures. For every attack that Satan would throw at me, my response was scripture. You need to learn to fight in the same manner. You need to fight to defend yourself, your family, your friends, and everyone from the attacks.

Your armor and your weapons come not from the world, but from the Father, and they have power unlike any other. Stand firm in the fight and deepen your faith in me, study and learn scriptures, live a righteous life, and experience the truth of salvation.

Lastly, always remember that you're not just to fight against things, but you are to fight for things. You are to fight for your marriage. You are to fight for your wife. You are to fight for your children. You are to fight for yourself. You are to fight for those who cannot fight for themselves. You are to fight for all that is good and loving in your life. You are to fight for the truth. That is the fight of a warrior in my army, that is what I want from you as one of my warriors. I want you to fight the good fight.

Scriptures:

1 Timothy 6:12 "Fight the good fight for the true faith. Hold tightly to the eternal life to which God has called you, which you have declared so well before many witnesses."
Ephesians 6:12-13 "For we are not fighting against flesh-and-blood enemies, but against evil rulers and authorities of the unseen world, against mighty powers in this dark world, and against evil spirits in the heavenly places. Therefore, put on every piece of God's armor so you will be able to resist the enemy in the time of evil. Then after the battle you will be standing firm."
1 Timothy 1:18-19 "Timothy, my son, here are my instructions for you, based on the prophetic words spoken about you earlier. May they help you fight well in the Lord's battles. Cling to your faith in Christ, and keep your conscience clear. For some people have deliberately violated their consciences; as a result, their faith has been shipwrecked."
Hebrews 4:12 "For the word of God is alive and powerful. It is sharper than the sharpest two-edged sword, cutting between soul and spirit, between joint and marrow..."

Questions: In what ways are you training to become a Warrior like Jesus? How will you improve your knowledge and use of the armor and weapons that were created for you?

THE FOUNDATION

From the old testament to the new testament, there is so much wisdom in the Bible. For someone who has read the Bible often, it's amazing how new all the books can seem. But, for someone who is new to the faith, it's overwhelming to try and absorb everything all at once. For those people who are new, or returning, to the faith, what is one of the most important things for them to learn?

Jesus: I've been asked this question, in various forms, many times over the years. In a short one-word answer, the foundation upon which all things are built is love. Love. Without love, all things crumble, and with love all things are possible.

You are to love openly and freely, without conditions. You are to love when you receive nothing in return from the other person. You are to love even when you disapprove of, or when you know that, the actions of the other person are not righteous or are even immoral, you are still to love.

You are to love God the Father with every aspect of your being. You are to love him with your heart, with your mind, and with your soul. You are to love him.

You are to love your neighbor. I know that this can be difficult, with garage door openers, and with people choosing to remain inside so much, however, those difficulties must be overcome. Get to know your neighbors and show them love.

You are to love your enemies. I know that this can be even more difficult. As with our earlier discussion on forgiveness, this is something for you and for them. And, always remember that your love towards your enemies has nothing to do with any judgment from the Father towards them.

You are to love yourself. This is not being selfish; this is following what I have taught. You are to love others as you love yourself. If you do not love yourself, you will have a difficult time loving others or loving the Father fully.

That's the foundation, the most important thing: to live a life of love. Everything else comes after that.

Scripture:

Matthew 22:37-40 "Jesus replied, 'You must love the Lord your God with all your heart, all your soul, and all your mind. This is the first and greatest commandment. A second is equally important: 'Love your neighbor as yourself.' The entire law and all the demands of the prophets are based on these two commandments."

John 13:34-35 "So now I am giving you a new commandment: Love each other. Just as I have loved you, you should love each other. Your love for one another will prove to the world that you are my disciples."

Hebrews 13:1-2 "Keep on loving each other as brothers and sisters. Don't forget to show hospitality to strangers, for some who have done this have entertained angels without realizing it!"

Matthew 5:44 "But I say, love your enemies! Pray for those who persecute you!"

Questions: What does it look like, and feel like, for you to love God with your heart, your mind, and your soul? In what ways can you show love for your neighbors, beyond what you are currently doing? How will you improve loving yourself?

YOUR MISSION

I wish this conversation could go on forever, listening to you and learning from you is an amazing experience. As we wrap up today, I'd like to know what I should do next, as a man. What should my mission be now, as I go out into the world?

Jesus: On the surface, this is a simple question with a simple answer: you are to love. You are to love the Father. You are to love everyone. You are to lead others to me. You are to share the Good News about me and the Father.

On the next level deeper, I want you to study and learn the scriptures more. But, not just in an academic sense, rather in a practical sense. Allow the word to flow through you in how you live your life as a light in the darkness. I want you to live so that your life is an example to others.

I want you to pray to the Father more. I want you to include me in your life more. I want you to surrender yourself and your ego and to live your life with me.

I want you to be willing to stand up for me in difficult situations. I want you to forgive those who have hurt you. I want you to forgive your enemies. I want you to forgive yourself.

I want you to seek out mentors and to be a mentor. I want you to seek out friends and to be a friend.

I want you to build a relationship with me, and to grow that relationship deeper all the time.

And always remember, the conversation can go on forever. I'll always be here waiting to pick this up and deepen our relationship. Anytime you're ready; I'm ready. So shall we begin?

Scriptures:

Matthew 28:18-20 "Jesus came and told his disciples, 'I have been given all authority in heaven and on earth. Therefore, go and make disciples of all the nations, baptizing them in the name of the Father and the Son and the Holy Spirit. Teach these new disciples to obey all the commands I have given you. And be sure of this: I am with you always, even to the end of the age."

John 17:20 "I am praying not only for these disciples by also for all who will ever believe in me through their message."

Matthew 4:19 "And he said to them, 'Follow me, and I will make you fishers of men.'" (ESV)

2 Timothy 1:8-10 "So never be ashamed to tell others about our Lord. And don't be ashamed of me, either, even though I'm in prison for him. With the strength God gives you, be ready to suffer with me for the sake of the Good News. For God saved us and called us to live a holy life. He did this, not because we deserved it, but because that was his plan from before the beginning of time – to show us his grace through Christ Jesus. And now he has made all of this plain to us by the appearing of Christ Jesus, our Savior. He broke the power of death and illuminated the way to life and immortality through the Good News.

John 13:34-35 "So now I am giving you a new commandment: Love each other. Just as I have loved you, you should love each other. Your love for one another will prove to the world that you are my disciples."

Questions: Are you ready to accept the mission you were given? Are you ready to be a fisher of men? Are you ready to live a life that demands an explanation? If so, how will you do that?

Final Notes

About the Author

Warren Peterson is a husband, father, son, brother, uncle, nephew, friend, author, entrepreneur, and mentor who is passionate about serving others.

Warren loves writing, public speaking, and leading people, often with deep questions they may have never considered before. His writing style isn't technical, it is very conversational, very personal, and is designed for everyone to read.

Warren enjoys traveling, has family all over the world, is happily married, and has four children with his amazing wife. When he needs a break, Warren loves getting away in the Rocky Mountains.

After the painful loss of his home, business, income, life savings, and even his own identity as a man, Warren determined to use his experience and calling to help others.

He founded Significant Man, an organization focused on leading men towards becoming the fathers, husbands, and leaders they were created to be. He loves teaching and mentoring men, seeing the changes in their lives, and the positive results in their families.

His personal verse is Titus 2:7-8, which reads: "Show yourself in all respects to be a model of good works, and in your teaching show integrity, dignity, and sound speech that cannot be condemned, so that an opponent may be put to shame, having nothing evil to say about us." (ESV)

To learn more about Warren, and his work, please visit him online at:

http://www.SignificantMan.com/about-warren

If *Jesus Man to Man* Has had a positive impact on you, please leave a review on Amazon for other readers.

If you would like to share how this book has impacted you directly with Warren, please email your personal story to Warren:
Story@WarrenPeterson.com

More from Warren

If you enjoyed this book, you might like these other books from Warren.

Becoming a Significant Man

Non-fiction book available now online and in bookstores.

The reality is that men have been sold a lie; they have been told that if they chase success in the world, then everything will be ok. Instead, they end up with the cars, the house, the toys, and are still left in pain asking, "Is this all there is?" The cost of the lie is enormous.

Becoming a Significant Man provides easy to digest ways on how to become the man you want to be and stay there. If you are tired of sleepwalking your way through life, then *Becoming a Significant Man is for you*. Warren Peterson, the founder of Significant Man, is eager for all men who have fallen behind in the game of life to benefit from his unique and powerful message.

Haven't you had enough? Enough of the struggle? Enough of feeling lost, without direction, and without hope? No more lies. No more pretending.

Your time is now. You have the power and permission to stand up and scream the truth about who you are— the significant man you were created to be!

Today Daddy?

"You were created with that power."

Today Daddy?

WARREN PETERSON
Author of *Becoming a Significant Man*

Fictional short story available now on Amazon.

Can one conversation change your life?

Joe Williams is a good man who works hard, loves his family, and is passionate about his hobby of restoring old cars.

Following the unexpected death of his daughter, Joe is struggling as a husband, as a father, and as a man.

Early one morning, when he cannot sleep, Joe takes a walk and has a chance encounter with an old Mechanic. The Mechanic forces Joe to tackle the ageless question, "Why did God allow this to happen?" "Every day, every moment, you have a choice to make. You were created with that power. Now what you do with that power, and what the rest of your life will be like, well, that part's up to you."

Reader Reviews for *Today Daddy?*

"This is one of the most hard-hitting, emotional stories I've ever read and it has really motivated me further to not take any moment I have with my wife or kids for granted. Make sure you're sitting down and have a box of tissues handy when you read this and be prepared for it to change your life forever."

"I challenge everyone to read this. It's a 52-page, tear-jerker of a story. If you don't at least get teary-eyed, I might question your humanity. It serves as a harsh reminder to never put off until tomorrow what can be done today. Make time to play with your children. Tell someone you care, even if you're angry with them. Don't lose sight of the beauty of the present moment. Soften your heart. Warren Peterson, you did a masterful job writing this. I can't recommend it enough."

"This story really made me rethink my priorities. They are easy to get confused. Want to bring yours into perspective? Take time to read this story!"

"This has been the most powerful, and at the same time the most simple, parenting book I've ever read."

Reader Reviews for *Becoming a Significant Man*

"This book is a must read for every man, especially fathers. It's packed with actionable strategies and ways to change your mindset to live a life of significance for your family. The chapters are short enough to get through in just a few minutes, and it's not weighed down by theoretical "fluff" like a lot of books in this genre can be. It's a gut punch to your soul that will make you a better version of yourself if you take it and act on it."

"Great Book. Warren Peterson continues to amaze me. If you're looking to make a change and want to become the best version of you, I highly recommend this book."

"This is a very useful book. Written from a Christian perspective (but not written as just for the faithful), it's a sincere and vulnerable look at what most men struggle with in terms of significance in their lives. We all make the mistake of thinking material gain, status, love, leisure and all manner of pursuits will fulfill us, only to attain one of those goals and not be fulfilled. Peterson takes the reader through the roadblocks and challenges that men face day to day, and offers constructive guidance on breaking through. Not trite platitudes, not gung-ho modern men's movement tripe, but very solid guidance presented with authenticity. Very highly recommended!"

Printed in Great Britain
by Amazon

60275659R00125